PSYCHODYNAMIC COACHING

PSYCHODYNAMIC COACHING

Focus & Depth

Ulla Charlotte Beck

Routledge
Taylor & Francis Group

LONDON AND NEW YORK

First published in Danish in 2009 by
Hans Reitzels, Copenhagen as
Psykodynamisk Coaching—fokus & dybde

First published 2012 by Karnac Books Ltd.

Published 2018 by Routledge
2 Park Square, Milton Park, Abingdon, Oxon OX14 4RN
711 Third Avenue, New York, NY 10017, USA

Routledge is an imprint of the Taylor & Francis Group, an informa business

British Library Cataloguing in Publication Data

British Library Cataloguing in Publication Data

A C.I.P. for this book is available from the British Library

ISBN 9781855757677 (pbk)

Edited, designed and produced by The Studio Publishing Services Ltd
www.publishingservicesuk.co.uk
e-mail: studio@publishingservicesuk.co.uk

CONTENTS

Ulla Charlotte Beck is Cand. Mag. (Copenhagen University and Århus University Denmark), studied political science and psychology, and afterwards trained in leadership and administration, pedagogy/ teaching, psychotherapy, and as a psychoanalytic group analyst. She has worked in organizational psychology since 1982 and is a member of ISPSO, OPUS, GAS, and NAPSO. In 1987, she started her "one-woman-networking" independent consultancy company, specializing in working with organizational and personal development, leadership training, and organizational learning activities. She is a co-founder of OPU, a postgraduate programme in organizational psychology at the Institute of Group Analysis in Copenhagen, where she is a teacher and consultant. She is also an external lecturer at Roskilde University for the Masters programme in organizational psychology. She has been director and staff member for several group relation conferences since 1994, and she has been the academic responsible for the personal development in the professional leadership training of doctors in the Danish Medical Association for fifteen years. She is author, and co-author, of several articles and books on organizational psychology.

Introduction

> "I was really out of my depth then. But now I'm clean. I . . . I have found myself," [said Edie]. "Whatever that is supposed to mean," said Sonia sharply. "It's what everyone says. Anyone would think people could find their own 'selves', anywhere, just lying about waiting to be picked up"
>
> (Hustvedt, 2008)

In Siri Hustvedt's novel, Sonia, the young woman who represents the new generation, is scornful of the constant efforts of the age "to find oneself". As if it was supposed to be so easy, or as if it was supposed to be so attractive.

Can one find oneself? Can one change oneself? Can one develop oneself?

These are the inexorable, involuntary central questions when one has started out along the path of writing about psychodynamic coaching. My answer is no—and yes. *No*, because the core of a person is highly stable, formed at an early stage, and partially rooted in the biological starting point and the very earliest relationships. *Yes*, because we can learn to make allowances for ourselves. We can get to know ourselves, and make allowances for the way we are marked by history, patterns, and tendencies, automatic actions, valencies, and primitive desires. *Yes*, because we can learn to read the world around us realistically and partially separated from our projections. We can find ourselves, so that we can become ourselves, or, in other words, create harmony between ourselves and the life we want to live. But it is not easy. It is hard, soul-searching, thought-sifting, and reflective work. It is frustrating and difficult. Real personal development is not all fun and games, no matter how the idea is sold. This book was written with a desire to create realism and seriousness about what coaching can be if it is really going to lead to development.

Psychodynamic coaching is not therapy, and the objective is not to examine the client's underlying problem and bring healing. Neither can psychodynamic coaching be compared with the superficial lifestyle coaching we meet in women's magazines, books on self-help, and on facile courses in the world of management, because, in contrast to these, it is filled out by solid theoretical knowledge and practice. Psychodynamic coaching is a process that forges a link between the client's past and present as a foundation on which to build a desirable and realistic future. Psychodynamic coaching has both focus and depth. This book outlines essential sections of psychodynamic theory, describes psychodynamic coaching, and illustrates it through cases. The cases and examples all derive from real courses of events, but are rewritten and altered so that they cannot be recognized. This is, of course, for reasons of discretion, but also to bring them in line with the didactic objectives of the book. I would, therefore, like to express my thanks to all the clients who have trustfully contributed over the years to my experience.

The first chapter sets out and specifies the objectives of the book and its starting point. The need for a description of psychodynamic coaching arises from a critical review of the existing schools of thought in coaching, and their non-existent, confused, or weak theoretical foundations. The connection between the associated psychodynamic theories is illustrated in a diagram, which also serves to give the book its structure. It is a defence of the suitability of the psychodynamic theory in connection with coaching processes.

The second chapter describes and underpins the model and the role of the coach. The model and role are illustrated continually in a case that is followed through. The figure from the first chapter also serves as an illustration of the various theoretical areas that the coach must be familiar with, and must bear in mind in any course of coaching.

The third chapter is a review of the relevant personality–psychological and developmental psychological theories that play a large part in individual coaching, but which also form the background for coaching pairs or groups. These are selected reviews, and far from comprehensive. The principle criterion for selection has been importance in connection with psychodynamic coaching. The theoretical summaries are included because it is important to emphasize how closely theory and practice are connected. When interpretations and ways of understanding are to be shared with the client, they must be firmly founded on theory, and not simply creative fantasy. The theoretic reviews are followed up by illustrative cases.

Chapter Four focuses on psychodynamic coaching of couples. Relevant—and, once again, selected—reviews of psychodynamic theories and concepts of the psychology of encounter are examined. Central concepts are highlighted and their value in application is illustrated in a case.

The fifth chapter deals with psychodynamic coaching of groups. This chapter, too, contains a selection of concepts that are central to coaching and presentations of relevant theories. A case illustrates how a course of psychodynamic coaching can progress in a working group, and how the perspective of a system is a central element in psychodynamic coaching.

Chapter Six deals with coaching in organizations. It explains when coaching can be relevant as part of organizational intervention or a management development programme.

Chapter Seven, which rounds off the book, compares different psychodynamic methods. The aim of this is to delineate psychodynamic coaching as one independent method among several. The book can be read from the beginning, following the order of the chapters. This will give a line of approach following the diagram in Chapter One, in a structured progression. The chapters can also be read independently, if the reader is interested in particular areas. However, reading the book in this way will mean losing the co-ordination of the parts and overview. A third way to read the book is to start with the last chapter and then continue with Chapter One. It might well suit some readers to place psychodynamic coaching in relation to other methods before reading about the actual content of psychodynamic coaching.

Writing a book with the purpose of establishing the form of a new phenomenon is not all fun and games. It felt like taking a risk to challenge both established psychoanalysis and the coaching industry. It was risky to volunteer to define what psychodynamic coaching is. At times, it has brought to mind Bion's words (although without any other point of similarity whatsoever) on the fate sometimes suffered by that kind of initiative: "Loaded with honour. Sunk without trace." That describes the anxiety. Yet, the project was not strangled at birth, but borne up by the drive to create and challenge, and the hope of inspiring others triumphed.

For various reasons, I have been met with mixed reactions when I have told people about the project of writing this book. Creativity does not only bring out enthusiasm. Organizational psychology is also a product with its own market and competition. That has taught me to tread cautiously at times. To be fair, I must say I have most often been met by knowledgeable people who have considered it a good idea, have encouraged and supported me, and regularly shown positive curiosity about it. It has been stimulating to be supported in carrying out an idea that had been so long in the making. I have been quite undeservedly lucky to be surrounded with people like that. First and foremost, I must thank my husband, Jens Gammelgaard. The simple truth is that, without him, there would have been no book at all. His chosen attitude has been support in every conceivable manner, practical or abstract, during my work. Thanks to my four children, Emma, Marie, Andreas, and Adam, who are no longer children. Thank you for your encouragement along the way and for your patience when work on the book has borrowed heavily from the time we shared.

Thanks to my colleague, psychiatrist and consultant Dr Torben Heinskou, who agreed unconditionally from the start to act as my sparring partner, as a professional reader and critic of parts of the manuscript. He has provided some excellent professional inspiration and both approval and criticism as the work progressed, both of which have improved the results. In spring 2008, I was invited to lead a two-day workshop at A. K. Rice's symposium in Chicago, entitled: "Leadership across the globe: transforming organizations and relationships". The title of the workshop was: "Psychodynamic coaching". As a result of the preparatory work and the inspiration from carrying out the workshop, I wished to structure the book differently and to make some changes in its content, which delayed the manuscript. My original publisher, Henning Persson, was very magnanimous in that connection, for which I am very grateful, but I would like to thank him in particular for believing in the idea from the start.

Ulla Charlotte Beck
Sorø, Denmark

CHAPTER ONE

Psychodynamics and coaching: why?

The purpose of this book is to put together an integrated picture of how it is possible to work through coaching based on a psychodynamic framework of understanding: psychodynamic coaching.

This book is for readers of three types:

- the curious reader who wants to know what psychodynamic coaching is;
- the reader who already knows a little, or perhaps more than just a little, about psychodynamic theory, and would like to know how it can be combined with coaching;
- the reader who knows a little, or more than a little, about coaching, and would like to know how it can be combined with solid theory and a serious conceptual approach.

Any reader who expects a complete overview of psychodynamic theory or of applied coaching will be disappointed. The material has been researched, some of it selected for inclusion, and some rejected. Coaching and psychodynamics are both overwhelming fields, and it would be unrealistically ambitious to attempt to embrace "everything". My choices were predominantly based on: (1) what I have gained many years of experience of through practising it; (2) what has worked and, thus, proved meaningful professionally; (3) what I have personally enjoyed, benefited from, and drawn satisfaction from working with; (4) what I believe others—students, participants on courses, colleagues, clients, and competitors—can benefit from.

Psychodynamic theory derives from psychoanalysis, the roots of which can be traced back to Freud at the beginning of the twentieth century, although Freud himself never used the expression "psychodynamic", calling it "dynamic" instead (Olsen, 2002). Coaching as we know it today is a newer phenomenon, dating back to the mid-1970s, originally targeted at sports performances. So, why this integration now? The good reason is that it adds value to both. The psychodynamic approach adds depth, effect, and seriousness to coaching. Coaching contributes with focus, structure, and drive. Jointly, they provide a unique opportunity for realistic changes with a basis in deep understanding. *The purpose of psychodynamic coaching is that the person being coached (the client), through acknowledgement and insight into his or her own history, personal patterns, inner structure, and the present context and its dynamics, can combine past, present, and wishes for the future with realistic, feasible actions.* That is an ambitious purpose, both in breadth and in depth. In breadth because it concerns the client's entire life (working life and personal life), including relations and circumstances, both current and past. This means that psychodynamic coaching is very different from the "lifestyle coaching" or "business coaching" we hear so much about in the media. In personal development work, it makes no sense to divide working life from personal life. We have our "selves" with us in both situations, and even though, on the face of it, different parts of the self move into the foreground depending on the context, other parts of the self are always present in the background. In depth because the psychodynamic investigative method of work seeks both back in time and "down" or "into" the client's unconscious, because an individual's motive for that person's way of living life is hidden in the unconscious. The innermost feelings, memories, fantasies, convictions, associations, and transference patterns are the data with which we can make contact with the unconscious material. The investigative work consists of observing, interpreting, forming hypotheses, and then testing these. The "then and when" is included in the "here and now". The investigative work takes place within the coach as well as the client and in joint collaboration between coach and client, at one and the same time. We will return to this in different ways in the following chapters.

Previously, I have sought to create clarity within the extensive field called coaching, supervision, role analysis, mentoring, personal development, etc. (Beck, 2004). All methods are engaged in creating development and/or learning on the personal level primarily in connection with, or based on, working life. The concepts are used at random and there is no consistency or logic in the way they are used. Users find themselves in an impenetrable jungle in this field. Nobody knows what they will get before they get it. The users, and this means both clients, who receive personal development/supervision/coaching, and those who provide coaching (and they have to learn it), for instance students, course participants, or consultants in private practice. The way coaching is "labelled", which can be studied in advertisements, catalogues, educational offers, websites, and books, does nothing to reduce the uncertainty. Well, the object of the intervention is ourselves, our (and other people's) very private "me", our personality, so this lack of clarity may have serious consequences. For both professional and ethical reasons, I feel very strongly about working to try to clarify this field and to identify a qualified alternative to the present situation. In my work from 2004, I set up some criteria for the type of practice (Beck, 2004, pp. 319–324) that is to characterize a new hybrid method between supervision and coaching. These criteria are set out below in a shortened form.

1. The method must refer to an organizational understanding, which includes an understanding of roles and an understanding of the significance of the task. It must be a model that comprises an understanding of the transport of unconscious material at different levels.

2. The method must contain an understanding of personality psychology that makes it possible to investigate personal patterns and the background for the projections that take place in the organization.

3. The method must provide the possibility of working on a specific personal issue for a limited time.

4. The method must provide the possibility of working in relation to general issues.

5. The method must be able to stand alone and not merely in an educational context.
6. The method must be "easy", uncomplicated.
7. The method must contain a resistance concept and principles for understanding and working with resistance
8. The consultant works from a neutral position. However, this is impossible in practice (and, no matter what, the consultant also has an unconscious in play), and, therefore, can only be aspired to as a target. The method must, therefore, include work with transference and countertransference.

If we combine the psychodynamic theory with the practice existing in psychoanalysis, group analysis, couples therapy, supervision, role analysis, personal development groups, and coaching, we then have an abundant selection of what the contents of this "hybrid" can consist. It is called *psychodynamic coaching*.

An integration of that kind is a daring venture that requires a dogma-free approach to the psychodynamic theory complex, the psychoanalytic tradition, the psychodynamic working methods, and to the many market-orientated methods for personal development that have popped up during the past couple of decades. An integration of that type will probably cause offence. There might, perhaps, be clever theorists and clinicians who will claim and prove that there would be built-in conflicts which would impair the quality of the actual psychoanalytical work; there might be precocious business-orientated commercial psychologists and consultants who would maintain that it is much too heavy and complex, or therapy-like and problem-orientated (with too negative an approach) to produce results. Looking at it from their point of view, they would be right. However, that is the consequence of working free of dogma. The reward—and the hope—is that there will be a real alternative and that it can lead to debate in professional life and, thus, to qualified further development both theoretically and in practice.

Psychodynamic theory

What separates psychodynamic theory from other theories, and is unique and exclusive, is the concept of the unconscious. Psychodynamic theories emphasize the importance of our unconscious mental life. One often encounters the mistaken idea that it is interest in the emotions that characterizes psychodynamic theory. However, there are many schools of psychology that focus on emotions, both those of the individual and as atmospheres in groups and environments or working and family cultures. In psychodynamic theory, emotions are data about the inner mental life, and it is in that perspective—as the informants from the unconscious—that emotions must be understood. Emotions are, therefore, important in psychodynamic theory, just as in other theories, although the distinguishing, characteristic aspect is the way in which feelings, together with conceptions, fantasies, thought, and language, are understood separately and also as they interact. The term "psychodynamic" is found in many psychological models. Psychodynamics is a collective term for all the models and descriptions of the psyche that are primarily preoccupied with unconscious processes. Olsen (2002) describes the special aspect of psychodynamic theories as the fact that they operate with "non-intended motive transformations (changes, distortions, redirections of instinctual impulses, desires or intentions) which can be analysed psychologically" (p. 5). It is the original motives that are repressed, which means they make their appearance in a distorted manifestation, which can be interpreted. It is the original motives that are relegated to the unconscious.

Olsen (p. 648) goes on to define psychodynamic psychology as the part of dynamic psychology that is based on therapy and has Freudian psychoanalysis as its clear foundation. The link between theory and practice is already embedded at the stage of definition. It is interesting to note that while the psychodynamic theories are, in fact, a well delineated phenomenon, at the same time the technical language associated with the theories has also become part of everyday communications. For instance, we use words such as "unconscious" and "ego" in daily speech, without necessarily being able to explain the underlying idea behind the concepts. Perhaps this tells us something about the impact of the psychodynamic theories, even though there have been numerous attempts at killing psychoanalysis, that is, rejecting it for the benefit of cognitive, constructionist, biological, or other approaches.

Within the psychodynamic theories there are theories and models that focus on various object fields. The criteria mentioned above for a "hybrid" are amply fulfilled. Psychodynamic theory includes theoretical sub-disciplines about personality, development, groups, including social psychology, leadership, role, organization, and about phenomena such as resistance and relations. These areas will be dealt with separately in the following chapters. Through the years, psychodynamic theory has developed in many directions and has created independent approaches, both conceptual and practical. Throughout history, some theories have come to terms with previous or present claims and, through criticism, have developed into new aspects and perspectives. Some theories have followed their own paths and deviate on a large number of issues from other parts of psychodynamic theories. They have founded new individual schools that share the same basic beliefs. In this book, some specific theories have been selected, which means some schools and approaches have been excluded, although in other circumstances they would have been included.

Coaching

Unlike psychodynamic theory, coaching is difficult to define as a category, and constitutes a very imprecise name for a lot of different work aimed at personal development and performance. The amount of literature on the subject is astounding. Much of the existing written material is actually marketing to promote the firms of consultants and individuals instead of providing theoretical and methodical material for development and clarification. There is nothing wrong with that; businesses and companies have every right to advertise, draw attention to themselves on the market, and make money. However, the difficulty lies in the fact that it is quite confusing for anyone with an ambition to create clarity that we are talking about the same thing when we say *coach* and *coaching*. It could also be considered an ethical and professional problem that the definition of the concepts is, to an increasing extent, being taken over by private companies with their own interests at heart. Imagine the situation if the same applied to services in the generally acknowledged system of professional training, for instance, for medical or legal degrees. This field is, in Denmark at least, uncontrolled and without public supervision. Anyone can call himself/herself a coach and give coaching. As long as there are customers, the business will flourish. If you blindly believe in market mechanisms, a selection should leave only the "effective" and "desirable" ones behind. That does not happen, however, in a complex postmodern society, where the market is not transparent and there is almost explosive growth in the supply. In Denmark, the public sector has started to offer coaching as a separate service, or as part of a supplementary training, for example, in connection with government managerial courses. It appears that the consultant firms and the training courses are selling and practising the same things, but they are completely different in every conceivable way. So, it is an exciting and important challenge to try to establish clarity in the field. It is not possible to comment systematically or deal with all the books, brochures, CDs, and pamphlets about coaching. I have called the type of coaching that appears in weekly magazines lifestyle coaching. This is right at the "light" end of the scale, and will not be discussed here. In the descriptions of the more substantial versions there are three common features: (1) it is important to focus on the potentials and desires of the individual; (2) the aim is to set goals for these; (3) it is done by asking (the correct) questions, so the person being coached can find the answers within him/herself. The coach—through questions—is the mediator making it possible for the individual to release his/her true self, feel his/her truly genuine wishes for the future, then to find the energy to change and act and, thus, reach his/her goals. One can get the impression that the word coaching releases something magical, on the level of expectation, at least. One of the products being sold is the actual coaching, and the other is the training to become a coach. You can become a coach—a personal trainer, a problem solving coach—or you can integrate the coach's role into your managerial style. Various companies sell "training", where they themselves are the certifying authority. Actually, it is a form of autopoeisis, or professional inbreeding, carrying the risk of jeopardizing the health of the profession.

Coaching and the lack of theory

In most cases coaching is presented as theoryless, meaning without being associated with any theory whatsoever. There might be a few aspects that are reminiscent of social constructionism and cognitive methods. Sometimes, for instance, references are made to both social constructionism and cognitive psychology, while, at the same time, the coaching wants you to learn to hold back on your projections (a concept predominantly rooted in psychodynamics) so that you can see a "pure" view of the "world" and the "other". References are made to several very different and, in some places, incompatible theories within the same method. In addition, it might raise doubts about whether concepts like projections have been correctly understood. In the promotion of coaching, coaching seems on the one side very simple and on the other rather complex, which gives rise to a number of incompatibilities. The manner in which coaching is generally practised is theoryless, or should I say not aware of which conceptual understandings are embedded in the practice in question. Understanding and pre-understanding both exist, previous understandings on which the current understandings are based, even though there is no explicit theory. Understandings and pre-understandings exist in most cases as something that has not been reflected upon, cliché-like, without any mutually cogent and logical connections. The individual is seldom aware of his or her understandings and pre-understandings. However, that is not necessary, and for most people in their own daily lives it is all right and satisfying, but, in the case of professionally performed work, to which people entrust their life, body and soul, it is only reasonable to demand something more behind the active processes. The lack of theory also shows in the coach's role. If the coach is to act as a catalyst for the individual's personal development, then it is logical to see the coach as a neutral, professional sparring partner, who can use language as an advanced tool in conversation, asking the right or wrong questions, perhaps uncomfortable and confrontational questions, gradually getting to know the client's weak points, unconscious patterns, innermost desires, and potential. The coach and client must not have any other relationship with each other apart from the coach and client relationship. Other relational connections must be regarded as sources of error, which will have a disruptive effect on the work for development.

As a method used in corporate and personal development, coaching has, understandably enough, always been on the lookout for a psychological theory it can connect to. In the 1970s and 1980s, it was predominantly the transaction analysis (Deegan, 1979), which derives from gestalt psychology. Later on, several systemic and social-constructionist approaches emerged, and the majority of these have been included. It is a characteristic of the psychological discourses within these directions that they focus primarily on the individual. To put it simply, it can be said that these theories are based on the following: (1) language is an active tool that works both inwardly and outwardly; (2) truth is a construction; (3) all social spaces are constructed as such. The group and language appear as defining social space—and there might be a battle about the definition of power. It is not irrelevant which theory the coach seeks to include. The coaching in extension of the social–constructivist approach is (of course) defined by the underlying perception: if the truth I carry about myself and my opportunities is a social construction, then the way to develop is to (get help to) construct a new truth for myself. Similarly, cognitive practice has left its traces in coaching, where the initial work is with the client's thoughts, as these are regarded as the force that creates the client's emotions, states of mind, and subsequent actions.

In some connections, we might encounter the phenomenon of the leader as coach, or the coaching style of leadership. But can coaching be integrated into the role of leadership, where power and authority are also part of the relationship? If the management is part of the social space in which the "truth" is created, it is difficult to imagine that at the same time there can be a space where you can find inspiration, independence, and freedom for a new "truth". It would be possible to form the hypothesis that coaching in some companies is more of a socializing process because it has a predefined purpose: adaptation. How does the constructivist approach fit together with the fact that the coach is problem solving? Are all solutions equally good? Attainable and realistic? By being neutral, that is, by not taking a stand as to whether one thing is better than another, do you risk sending your client off on a Sisyphean task? Is any construction just as good as any other, regardless of whether the client breaks his/her neck carrying it out? My claim is that any practised coaching method is closely connected to the theoretical basis, both when it is absent and when it is present. It is understandable, therefore, that coaching and people working with coaching have been, and continue to be, on the lookout for an appropriate theory.

With the appearance of the book *Coaching—læring og udvikling* [Coaching—learning and development] (Stelter, 2002), a Danish attempt was made to place coaching as the authors practised it in a theoretical perspective. This book links coaching with systemic theory and the method of systemic dialogue. It makes it possible to investigate what significance the theoretical starting point has for the method. The book is a good example of the serious literature that exists on the subject, so it is worth commenting on it. A general thesis running through systemic-based coaching is that the owner of the problem also possesses the key to solving it (Hansen-Skovmoes & Rosenkvist, 2002, p. 85). This postulation forms the basis for coaching: it is the foundation on which coaching is built up. Nevertheless, there are people who, as a result of unconsciously generated patterns or their own abilities, do not possess this key. Their inner dynamics prevent them—even with the best questions and the best systemic coaches—from finding the key. In these cases, it is necessary to find a different explanatory model, which provides different possibilities for action.

From a psychodynamic perspective, these individuals can be understood as people whose history and some of their experiences mean that certain actions and possibilities do not exist. It might be because they are not meaningful or practicable, or because merely cognitive contact with the possible actions creates inner states of anxiety. States of anxiety like that might also be repressed from consciousness, because they, too, are threats. They are not threats in the general sense, but specifically for the particular person with the particular pattern. Anxiety here cannot be overcome and exploited positively. Another thesis in the book is that we each do what makes most sense to us. In my psychodynamic practice, I have encountered several clients who perform actions and whose behaviour cannot be said to be meaningful, seen from the outside. Perhaps not from the inside either, even from their own points of view. The obvious examples to visualize are the countless people who struggle to make choices, and especially choosing to do without. Again and again they say yes when it would have been more meaningful to say no—also in their own conscious understanding. This can have serious consequences, such as a state of dissatisfaction, frustration, and stress. Some people do not possess the ability to look after themselves; others are bound to deeply rooted inner forms of logic. Some are constantly getting into trouble because they are unable to "read" themselves or others. Or people who have an addiction (to alcohol, drugs, work, games, and/or other people) of some kind (we are discussing quite ordinary people here, with or without a special career, not people who are ill or dysfunctional), people who constantly end up in problematical relationships, or are unable to form stable relationships. They are following forms of logic that concern fundamental coherences that have been formed in childhood or at a young age. Some are aware of it, and realize that the point they have reached and their situation in life are defined more by something external or "other" than by their own essential needs. If we are to understand how these situations arise, we have to search for something more complex than the postulates above.

A third thesis is that distinguishing the problem from the person (Hansen-Skovmoes & Rosenkvist, 2002, p. 89) is a precondition for being able to acknowledge it and act. At first glance, it could appear that this thesis does not fit well with the previous thesis that we, as people, do what is most meaningful, because in that case, does it not mean that the problem is really myself and my "truth" about what provides the best meaning? In my opinion, the highly probable consequence of externalizing the problem in this way will also lead to an externalized solution, acknowledgement, and action. The psychodynamic position will present precisely the opportunity to acknowledge that it is *me* that has this problem because *I* have this pattern and this repetitive compulsive disorder, and the solution lies in working with its background. The responsibility for expanding my own opportunities in life could actually lie in acknowledging that it is connected to me and, therefore, possibly I am the person who can develop and free myself of it.

It is also possible that the interaction between the deeper underlying dynamics of the group, the family, or the place of work, or the organization at the place of work, and the individual person can become so complex that it can only be understood through a more complete analytical investigation. There are several more theses that could similarly be commented on. What is interesting is that in this way it becomes clear that theoretical understanding is of crucial importance for how the work can and will be performed. Systematic understanding attaches vital importance to seeing the problems in a circular perspective, and this is a contrast to the linear understanding of cause and effect. From a psychodynamic perspective one says "both ... and" instead of "either ... or", since there are connections that have to be understood linearly and connections that have to be understood as circular, and often they, too, are interconnected. We have patterns that can be understood as a combination of our biology and our very early childhood. Relations that have been experienced at an early age are internalized and are enacted later on in life's outer relations by means of our unconscious assistance. Our unconscious is co-producer of the "scenes" we take part in and experience around us. We experience situations in life that, on the face of it, seem completely different, but essentially are the same and provide us with the same insistent result: for instance, the feeling of incompetence. To put it simply, there are both linear and circular coherences between the patterns and problems we might have. Precisely because our repertoire is small, or our perception is limited, we contribute in a way that can wind us up in circular connections. The theoretical section of Selter's book is divided into two chapters: one that deals with management theory and one that deals with learning (Stelter, 2002, Chapters Six and Seven). Both chapters examine relevant, but very limited, theories in this field. Especially in relation to theories of learning, more could have been included. The absence of theory about development and personality seems problematical when it is intended as the background for a type of method-coaching—that not only involves learning and management, but also development, personality, organizations, group processes, etc. As illustrated here, the systemic model is too narrow, or else it becomes too narrow, because the models and concepts that actually exist are not put to use. And that is perhaps the point behind the lack of clarity: the interest in a theoretical basis is very slight. Perhaps it is everything about the phenomenon of coaching that is most interesting.

Why is it such a good idea to link psychodynamic theory with coaching?

It is a good idea to link psychodynamic theory with coaching because we are different, because we do not all have the same resources and potentials, either biologically, socially, or psychologically; because we do not have unlimited potential, but have our limitations, too; because, in a given situation, some things might be healthier than others; because it is not just the individual, but also the systems in which the individual is acting that are interesting, so we have to comprehend what takes place in co-relations in simple and complex relations and systems; because psychodynamic theory offers ways of understanding all this. Therefore, the psychodynamic approach provides the opportunity of practising coaching in other ways, methods that make allowances for this. Each of us is unique, and, therefore, unlike anyone else. Hence, each individual should also be given unique coaching; in principle, a separate little research process, with investigations based on the given data, where hypotheses are openly formed and worked with. This is because personal development is not *only* about the client finding "something" inside him/herself; personal development also means opening up possibilities. Catching sight of something outside yourself, in the other person or people and in the relationship. The relationship between the coach and client, or client group and coach, must lead to the creation of inner states of mind within the individual, similar to those where the original pattern was created. This is a prerequisite for the deep acknowledgement that makes it possible to remove inhibitions and become receptive to new possibilities, where possibilities are created for "Aha" experiences "here-and-now". That cannot be done through questions alone. With regard to these aspects, psychodynamic coaching is similar to therapeutic psychodynamic work, and psychoanalysis. Psychodynamic coaching works with structured exercises because the desired focus is more narrowly determined, contrary to psychoanalysis, for instance. Psychodynamic coaching is not therapy, but it can have a therapeutic effect.

Psychodynamic coaching

Following on from what I have said above, in this book I will use the term *coach* for the person with the professional role who is at work providing the coaching. The *client* is the term for the person at the receiving end of the coaching, the person who is present as "himself" or "herself", privately (also when it is primarily a work-related area that is to be worked on). If it is a group of clients, they are collectively called the *client group*. These terms might vary, depending on the context. For instance, in some educational situations, *consultant* and *participants* or *teacher* and *students* would apply. The psychodynamic theory provides the coach with a great many interpretations of, and insights into, various psychological fields. They, in turn, form the background for the work done by the coach. The client and the client's business are in focus in the foreground. In relation to the client and to the client's business, the coach works together with the client and alone with him/herself. At one and the same time, the coach is at work in his/her inner self and in the existing "now" with the client. It is an important quality for the coach to be able to divide attention and at the same time to be fully present in the immediate moment. It is often an advantage to be able to share this work with colleagues. In some cases, the coach's work-related context makes professional reflection possible, where colleagues can discuss and reflect on each other's work and "cases". It helps to qualify the work the coach does before, during, and after a coaching session.

A central aspect of the psychodynamic tradition is the work with the relationship between the client and the coach. There is an awareness of this in several methods, but the importance given to this relationship is quite specific for the psychodynamic method. The relationship is the medium through which the psychological change takes place. And that is why the relationship must be free of dependency. The concepts of transference and countertransference make it possible to understand and to work with the relationship in this sense. *Transference* is the term for the phenomenon when the client unconsciously plays back wishes and conflicts in his/her relation to the coach. That means the emotions, fantasies, and opinions that the client has had in relation to central persons in his/her life are redirected and repeated in relation to the coach. You could say that the client's unconscious is attempting to stage/gestalt an original relationship or the original relationship. There will be a corresponding *countertransference* on the part of the coach. Countertransference is the unconscious feelings and sentiments that arise in the coach during the coaching sessions. They disturb the coach in working with *freely floating attention*, which is the term for the desirable way in which the coach should listen to the client, an open and fully attentive way, without preconceived opinions or feelings. It is an ideal that is unlikely to be achieved one hundred per cent. On investigating his/her own countertransference, the coach receives data about the client's transference, as countertransference is a reaction to the transference relationship. Instead of attempting to control the countertransference, it is more important to be open and investigative towards it. Collegial supervision can be especially valuable for the work with countertransference, because colleagues can open up the coach's blind spots. In coaching, in contrast to therapy and psychoanalysis, there is a specific reason for the person initially contacting the coach.

Therapy and psychoanalysis can be regarded as an analysis of the entire person in question, perhaps with a view to recovery. In psychoanalysis, the client or patient is, in principle, saying, "Life hurts. Analyse all of me so I can get well, or, so I can handle my life that has become so difficult, or, so I can get to know myself better". The patient or the client will, of course, present a more specific formulation. In coaching, the client is saying, "Coach me, so I can handle my relations with certain situations/feelings/bosses/new sales targets/women/men/work/myself/employees, etc., in a better and more satisfactory way". This difference is vital because it is this that sets the framework for the way in which the work will be done. It is quite possible that the client will also come to know him/herself better or become "healthier" through the coaching, but that is not the primary reason for coming to the coach. It places demands on the coach's ability to work while maintaining focus and within a limited time. The coach must be able to tune in and use himself in a plastic way, as a tool for the process which is about to start. It is not expert consultancy but development work, which only can take place in specialized collaboration between client and coach.

The work starts when the client contacts the coach. Right from this beginning, there will be important data to note. Why did the client come? What is characteristic of the way the client made contact? What expectations and feelings are expressed? Is it easy or difficult to find time for an appointment? Is it the client him/herself that thinks coaching is a good idea? Does the client believe it will help, or is it just something to be tried out? And so on. Often it can be seen—with hindsight—that the whole story and pattern was presented when the client made the initial contact. The basis for coaching is the client's business: what is to be achieved by the coaching? When does the coaching start? What is the framework for the initial position? Was it the boss who granted ten coaching sessions because there are some co-operation issues? If so, what was the reason for doing so? Is the boss also a large or small part of the problem? Was it the client's own idea to seek help in a situation that includes both the role at work and that in personal life? Starting points might differ greatly. No matter what the starting point is, or the reason for contacting the coach, the coach must be able to relate, both in theory and in practice, to a very large complex, which is illustrated in Figure 1.

The model is to be understood as follows: at the centre is the individual, the well-nourished baby holding a diskette. The diskette symbolizes that some things are given right from birth. The equipment we have with us varies when we enter this world. To a certain extent, our biology determines our possibilities and limitations. Until birth, the mother's inner environment has formed the framework for the child, and at that time and later in life, the environment can add to and detract from the possibilities open to us. As soon as we are born and can breathe ourselves, the outer social, psychological, and physical environment begins exerting an effect. We are received by "the important other(s)". But how are we received? What is the significance of the things that happen? We live, and build up a story that marks us, together with our given starting points. Personality psychology and development psychology present possible ways of explaining and understanding at the individual level. We meet "the other" and the dynamics start to interact, with hope and fear, security and anxiety,

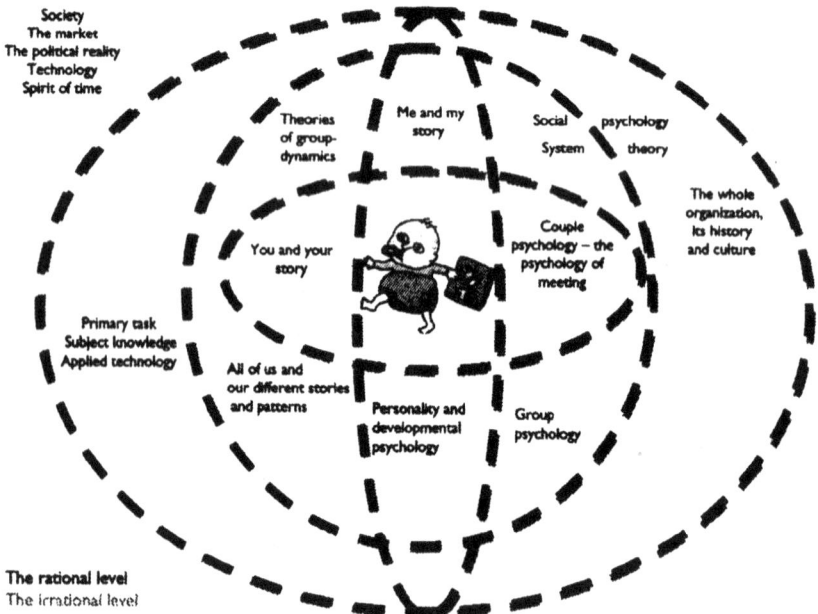

Figure 1.

love and hate, openness and closedness, happiness and disappointment, good or bad luck. Couple psychology, or the psychology of meeting, makes it possible to fathom what is going on in the relationship. We are members of groups, and perhaps we have always known about groups because we were born into a large family group. Both identity groups and task groups form a major part of most people's lives. From the first day at the crèche, we become members of various groups. A major part of life consists of communicating and interacting with other groups and internally within a group. Many individuals, and just as many stories, are brought into play, with lots of relationships, both rational and emotional. Well documented group psychology makes it possible to analyse and understand the interaction in a given group. Finally, most of us also form part of an organization. Work fills out much of life for a great many people, and in postmodern life changes are taking place in society and in working life at an accelerating rate, raising it to an increasing degree of complexity, both publicly and privately. We are directly and indirectly involved in the ongoing changes that affect us in various ways. We spend a lot of time in the organization, and it takes on importance and becomes a determining factor in other parts of our lives as well.

Organizational psychology, which has developed rapidly since the Second World War, deals with the psychology and the dynamics that are seen while we are at work. Management is an extremely well documented phenomenon. What importance do the tasks have that we work with? The organization has its own culture—what is its significance? At the outermost point of the model is political reality, the Market, Society, the Spirit of the Times. A rapidly changing society sets the agenda for many aspects of our lives. An attempt to grasp the consequences of events at the level of a whole society can be useful in understanding what you are dealing with yourself as part of a greater entity. Being able to see the connections between the various levels counteracts the experience of fragmentation. Social systems, that is, families, groups, workplaces, and society, have both a rational construction and a structure that we can describe. However, all social systems are also illogical and complex, too. They are driven by invisible circumstances and dynamics that appear as irrationality. All fields in the model can, thus, be studied at a rational and an irrational level, but especially the *interaction* between the rational and the irrational can bring greater clarity and create freer, and more realistic, possibilities.

For psychodynamic coaching, reality plays a part. There are limitations, there are things that are not feasible, and there are goals that only some can reach. Nevertheless, there are also a great many undiscovered possibilities, which suddenly come into existence and, indeed, become real possibilities when understanding has become deeper and the blind spots have become less blind. The starting point for psychodynamic coaching lies where the client's business is. If the client seeks coaching because the collaboration with a colleague is really bad and he/she now wishes to be coached in relation to that, then it is reasonable to start out from the area concerned with "the psychology of pairs—our dynamics". The "investigation" can begin there. The opening moves can take several forms: you can ask the client to give an account of all there is to tell, letting the client be responsible for doing the talking and telling you about his/her wishes for change; you can control the type of data you want to work with by asking questions in certain ways, or you can ask the client to draw the situation, or associate to the situation, etc. The coach might have his/her preferred modes of working and his/her reasons for these. It is important that the coach is aware that there lies something "before", historically speaking (the client's personal history), and something "after" the group in which the collaboration takes place, the organization and the context in which it exists, and there are the tasks as outlined in the model. In reality, it is, of course, present at the same time, so the model is to be used as a framework for methodical thinking as things progress, and also to keep the coach focused on the numerous connections and complexities the actual business has. Finally, there is the client's actual situation in life: is the client young and newly qualified, just married, in a steady relationship, divorced, a father/mother, single, with small children, older children that are leaving home, grown-up children and grandchildren, just returned from living abroad, chronically ill, won a lottery, has lost both parents, or what?

In our postmodern existence, we do not follow through the more traditional phases of life, but swap around more than previously. Increasing numbers get divorced, have several sets of children, live alone, choose not to have children, live globally, and so on and so forth. The form of life is more a choice than it used to be, rather than tradition or fate. How many areas of life the coaching spreads to can vary. In psychodynamic coaching, work is mainly concentrated on a limited theme and a defined goal for an agreed number of limited sessions. However, there can be derived forms: it can be a continuous process, where you work with your own development, and it can be part of supplementary training, where it primarily deals with the professional role in connection with the training in question. When it is important for the coach to understand possible connections with the other areas in the model, apart from the one chosen as the starting point, it is because comparing relations and situations from various areas might reveal surprising opportunities for acknowledgements. A good example of this is, during a supplementary training process, to create the possibility for the client—the student—to compare his/her role at work with his/her role in the family (both present and past) and again with his/her role in the training. This opens up an opportunity to investigate repetitions and patterns. If the work goes on in a group of co-students, or in a client group, additional "help" could come from the others in the group through feedback and associations.

In a one-to-one coaching situation, it can be rewarding to compare the client's account of important relations in his personal story with an account of working life relations, and then the relationship between the client and the coach. This triangulation makes the discoveries very convincing, as triangulation also does in scientific work. At the methodical level, psychodynamic coaching can find plenty of inspiration in other methods, and the systemic tradition in particular, with its different reflexive designs, has proved very inspiring. Based on knowledge and experience, the psychodynamic coach will continually form hypotheses about the client's repressed material and patterns. These hypotheses can be presented to the client, so that coach and client can work with them together. It is important to have a good idea of when to share your hypothesis with a client. The form in which it is presented is also important. Bad timing could result not just in stagnation, but also recession in the work, because when the hypothesis is presented, so much resistance might be created that it activates defence, which might possibly include the pattern with which you are working.

As previously mentioned, the coach gathers material—or data—to work on from the very first contact. All contact and communications are data. When the coaching is part of a course of coaching, there will be additional opportunities for meeting each other apart from the actual coaching sessions. The coach's inner "recording machine" runs all the time. That means that observations from breaks, presentations, group exercises, and the like are also data. The following is a brief case that illustrates how data proves to be usable and how the consultant might consider a "hypothesis" about the client's pattern of behaviour underlying the problem.

Case: John

John is on a course together with his colleagues. They are all middle managers in a large, privately owned company. Judging by John's appearance, he is a man who does not take care of his health. He is overweight, short of breath, and somehow looks untidy, although his clothes are expensive and exclusive. John speaks very fast and there is no mimic in his face. His complexion is unhealthy. (Due to high blood pressure?) The purpose of the course is to improve the collaboration in the managerial group through talks, exercises, and coaching, in groups and individually. In connection with the coaching, they must choose one of their issues where they would like to see some improvement, and try to understand why things are as they are, and thereby make it possible to create new ways for working together. This is what John has brought up: it annoys him that he can never get help from his colleagues when he is short of "people", that is, employees. He says that he always sends at least the amount of people the other departments ask him for when they are short-handed. He would like to support the joint cause, and would like "something in return" when he is in need of help. He likes the thought of somebody owing him favours. However, he never feels that he reaps any benefit from this kind of "saving up". While John gives his account, you can really feel how difficult it is for him. It is not just a practical, logistical problem, but also an emotional one. He feels rejected and treated as an outsider.

Giving his account of the problem takes John out of emotional control: he becomes upset in a way that not only surprises him but clearly makes an impression on the other members of the group. John attempts to hide the fact that he is out of balance by blowing his nose. The other members of the group are not from John's own department, and most of the time only remotely in contact with him and his department. A few are from the departments that do not provide

John with the help he wants. One of these, who, according to John's account, has become one of the ones that will not help him by returning favours, is sitting uneasily on his chair clenching and unclenching one hand. This is not particularly visible, but rather concealed under his jacket. He says nothing. The other person from one of the nearby departments sees it, but he, too, says nothing.

Afterwards, they all have a coffee break. There is a large plate of cakes on the table. John arrives a little later than the others, finds a seat, and stretches for the plate of cakes. He takes two and puts the cake plate down. My first thought is that it was rather rude of him, first, to take two cakes (as there were not that many cakes), and second, not to pass the plate around. My thought is probably based in my superego, as John's actions would not slip through my personal system. The thought remains as a thought and the registration of data. I connect this experience with John's account and the reactions I have seen in the group during his account. It contributes to a hypothesis that attempts to answer the questions: Why does John have this problem? In which way is John co-creator of his own problem? The data from the break, coupled with the reaction of the clenched hand in the group, make me think that other people experience John completely differently from the way he experiences himself. I draw up my hypothesis: *John is so afraid of not getting what is his that he takes it himself before anybody gets the chance to offer him anything.* The hypothesis remains a thought and an idea in my mind.

At the next group session, the others give their accounts of how they experience John daily. It appears that the members of the other departments do not feel they owe John anything. They are unable to comprehend his problem. One of them gives an account of how John, who arrives very early, together with "the people", has often been over to their departments and "borrowed" staff without asking the managers on the spot. A dialogue follows between John and the others about whether this is true and why it happens. Suddenly, one of the others exclaims, "I'm so sick and tired of your 'thieving' from me—I don't owe you anything at all!" John is offended and leaves the room. I find data confirming my hypothesis.

Later on, in a one-to-one coaching session with John, I present him with my hypothesis and all its data. At the same time, I add that, in relation to myself, I have experienced the same thing, and that on this occasion and the previous coaching session he arrived early and asked whether we could start right away. Then, when time is running out, he introduces new themes in order to prolong the session. It is difficult to get him to leave the room, and several times he says, "Oh, and by the way . . .", and "Ooh, I forgot to tell you—and it is important . . ." He keeps a hold on me with "interesting" new stories and clutching at the "now". It creates a feeling of irritation inside me. I find him greedy.

Confronted with the hypothesis and data about countertransference, it becomes possible to work deeper down in John's story and the feelings that are associated with it, and to investigate together where this pattern comes from. After the management course, which, in fact, offered opportunities for both personal development in management and coaching sessions in groups and individually, John was granted a course of eight two-hour coaching sessions. He managed to work in depth on the complex of problems that arose from his personal patterns and the dynamics of the organization. During the series of coaching sessions, he made considerable progress in personal development. It was demanding, and cost a lot of energy when he had to see and understand himself in a new light. It was painful to draw projections and paranoid conceptions back to himself, and it was difficult to feel how and why these patterns had developed. He had a great desire for "alleviation", and this gave him the strength of will to complete the course.

John was an example that confirmed how the desire for acknowledgement and working through feelings and experiences produces a release of psychic energy and creates space for other actions.

That is a simplified account of an actual event, but serves to illustrate how, in psychodynamic coaching, you can work together with the client towards "solving the case". Just like a detective. This form of work characterizes the psychodynamic method: it investigates, researches, and is prepared all the time to see new connections.

> Sigmund Freud, like Sherlock Holmes, was an interpreter of symptoms; he was also an interpreter of dreams, of fantasies, someone preoccupied with the meaning of the trivial, the inexplicable, the irrational. . . . Interpretation lies at the heart of psychoanalysis both as a research activity and as a clinical practice. [Gabriel, 1999, p. 251]

The model for psychodynamic coaching will be described in Chapter Two. The description is followed by an ongoing case that illustrates the various phases and shows how the content of this kind of "detective work" can unfold.

Psychodynamic coaching

In the following is a description of psychodynamic coaching in practice. The method consists of the following steps:

1. The client's first contact.
2. The first coaching session: objectives and framework.
3. The course of coaching.
4. Conclusion: evaluation and leave-taking.

This chapter will show how psychodynamic coaching means working actively with a direct focus on the client's business. The coach also carries out active, focused work indirectly, with him/herself as the receptive instrument for both conscious and unconscious processes that exist in the relationship, and in the parallel processes started up by what is told. It is through understanding these and working on the relationship that movement, change, and lasting development are created. When unconscious patterns and dynamics become conscious, it is possible to change them, or, if it is not possible to change them, it is possible to make adjustments in relation to them. When unconscious factors are made conscious, this is not purely due to cognitive insight or the establishment of understanding, but to a simultaneous, deeper, inner binding emotionally. Freud distinguishes between *pre-conscious* and *unconscious*, where the pre-conscious is what can become conscious only through an exertion of attention (Freud, 1915e). Even though Freud develops these concepts further to the actual hypothesis of psychic apparatus (Freud, 1923b), it is, in practice, meaningful to differentiate between the pre-conscious and the unconscious. The pre-conscious is less effectively repressed than the unconscious. Much personal development consists of making conscious what is pre-conscious. When there is no question of people suffering from actual dysfunction—or pathology—but from undesirable, frustrating, or unsatisfying situations within the normal range, uncovering pre-conscious factors can be very stimulating for development. It renders it possible to make conscious choices about changes in life. As defined in the introduction, the purpose of psychodynamic coaching is that the client, through acknowledgement and insight into his or her own history, personal patterns, inner structure, the present context and its dynamics, can combine past, present, and wishes for the future with realistic, feasible actions. The way to achieve this is a demanding process in which the pre-conscious and unconscious are awoken to consciousness.

The client's first contact

The first step in psychodynamic coaching is concerned with the first time the client makes contact. It is my experience, gained from many courses of coaching, that a great deal of information is already present at the first contact. The relationship, with its transference and countertransference, is under way. For this reason, it is well worth investing time and attention in taking notice and registering data right from the start. There is data that one first begins to understand later on in the process. What characterizes the meeting? What is the client's situation? Investigating? Prepared? Ready to make a start? Wretched? Conscious consumer? Sceptical? Curious? Embarrassed? Demanding? Finding it hard to wait? Does not really know? Why is the client asking for coaching? What is he/she expecting? Whose idea was it? Who is paying? What does the client know about coaching? Has someone referred him/her, or is this approach the outcome of more or less random searching on the Internet or in telephone books? If someone has passed on a name, who was it? And what is their relationship? Is the client making demands on the practical arrangements—for instance, only after working hours, or only four sessions, or anything else? It is important to be aware of the countertransference situation from the start. Which voices, conceptions, and fantasies arise from contact with the client?

Case: Karen

Karen sends me an e-mail, enquiring whether she can make an appointment. She informs me in the e-mail that she is the leader of a large secretariat, where a major change in the organization has just been implemented, in the course of which it was necessary to transfer some employees against their wishes. The new structure is now in place, and she thinks it went well, all in all, but she is surprised to find that in her mind she keeps going back to the events involving the employees who were forced to "swallow some camels", as she puts it. They were transferred to other jobs unwillingly and against their wishes. She would like to talk it over, because she feels it takes up far too much energy to go round with it on her mind. "It cannot be changed now, and there will be more of that kind of process in the future, so I will have to learn to deal with it." She asks how few hours I think we can make do with to deal with this "issue".

If we return to the illustration from Chapter One, we can immediately see that the following areas are involved:

> Karen as an individual: from the perspective of personality and developmental psychology.
> Karen meeting "the other": the employees who were forced to "swallow camels" and managers and superiors who initiated the change, or, in other words, the psychology of meeting and relations with authorities.
> The organization as the background against which the events described took place.
> Karen's role in the organization—and here, too, are relations with authorities.
> Karen as one of the "secretariat" group: group psychology.

When Karen and I meet, it is not only a meeting between the two of us, but the system Karen works in is also represented in what Karen tells me. In the telling, material from the system is transferred uncon-sciously. This is one of the strengths of psychodynamic coaching: it looks at more than the client in isolation. The work is not fixated in individualization. Clients always bring more than themselves and their goals for coaching. The client and the goal appear in context, in a system. It might be the family as a system, groups from their work-ing lives, their free time, workplaces or the organizational system, and it might arise from the dynamics of assignments.

I phone Karen and we make an appointment, and prepare for the first session.

Immediately after the interview, I write down my conceptions and fantasies, no matter how prejudiced, subjective, groundless, or unpro-fessional they might be (see Appendix 1). They may be associated with the voice, the choice of words, the mood, or what kinds of attitudes I imagine the client "goes in for". What do I think she looks like? What knowledge and ideas do I have about the organization she works for and her job? Its name? Expectations about the course of coaching? Do I think I know already what it is all about? What feelings are produced in me immediately? I know Karen's organization from previous assignments and enquiries, so I know that she is in an extremely diffi-cult organization. There have been many structural changes in recent years. They are under pressure because the budget is repeatedly exceeded, and from management changes at the top levels. One of its characteristics is lack of human consideration: the budget always comes first, no matter what, and if mistakes are made, energy is spent on finding a culprit, who is then dismissed.

Here are some of the points I wrote down.

What does it mean when I know the organization and judge it in that way? It is difficult to get an idea of Karen's age. There is some-thing young as well as something older about her. This is not her first job in leadership. She is efficient, ambitious, and perhaps something of a perfectionist. Karen gives the impression of being most comfort-able with rational and linear interpretations and solutions. She has little interest in psychology: it is as if it irritates her when things do not work out. Her enquiry gives the impression of being properly organized on the lines of "I am in control of everything, apart from this one 'issue', but I have almost got that sorted too, or I will have as soon as possible." I feel an idea pressing down on me. If she does not get this under control in a flash, it is probably because I am the one who is not good enough at my job. The use of the word "issue" gives me a sensation of wishing to keep emotions away from what it is all about. Something annoying has cropped up, and it must be dealt with. How can she say that the organizational restructuring is "in place"? That sort of thing usually takes a long time to fall into place. I imagine her attitude as something like "It can't be that difficult, surely?", demonstrating a lack of understanding for the psychological aspects. Inner picture: she is super-organized, cool, childless, and career minded. Prejudiced—but where do I get that from? On the other hand, she does mention that she keeps going back to the events involving the employees who were transferred. The voice on the telephone also gave me that "double" sensation. Does it have anything to do with the organization? Are her defences about to go down? So, she is beginning to feel some dilemmas: for instance, how difficult it *really* is to be there and as the leader be partially responsible for the decisions from above and their success. Why does she find it *so* difficult?

As can clearly be seen, my impressions are full of prejudices, and there is very little basis for some of the conclusions. There are projections in play from my side. I distance myself from being unfeeling, from being one hundred per cent career minded, from childlessness, and from unreflecting desires for efficiency and being too naïve about how long processes of change really take. I am reaching immediate conclusions from previous experiences with the organization. One risk might be that I begin to see Karen as a "victim", moulded by the organizational culture, or even as someone actually chosen because she fitted well into the organizational culture. By jotting things down in such an uncensored and unsystematic manner, I make contact with all that is being activated in me. I can re-read and reflect on it, and I can catch sight of what and how much I am putting into the work and the relationship. In that way, I prepare for the first session. While re-reading what I wrote down here, I was struck by a feeling of unease, which it took me some time to put into words. What was happening was that it activated my own feelings from earlier on about being in competition with women, competition where I had been the loser, because I was unable to read the game, and because I was far too naïve. Could there be an element of gender and womanliness at the root of it here? I do not know what set it off, but something did.

Reflection about what is written down makes it possible for me to be aware of my own unconscious dynamics or those in the relationship, and, thus, I am prevented from acting on them directly or without reflection. I am better able to put it all behind me and thus reduce the effect. This makes it possible to be free from ideas arising immediately inside me, so that I can really be more curious about *what* it could be that awoke all these feelings in me. What does it tell me about the situation itself, about how Karen's colleagues have perceived her, about the attitudes she might have assumed in order to be able to cope with the assignment of making changes, about her inner images and emotional conceptions of what is possible and desirable in the organization? These are factors that it might also be necessary for Karen to investigate herself during the coaching. What are Karen's conscious and unconscious contributions to the situation, and how do they interact with the contributions from the various other people and systems?

I am not at all exceptional with regard to the thoughts and feelings that arise, even after such a short contact. We all react in many ways to establishing a new relationship, some of which we are not necessarily proud of. It is not possible for any of us, regardless of experience and training, to cleanse ourselves of these conceptions without working on them consciously. If we do not work consciously with our countertransferences and our pre-conscious conceptions, our experience could even seduce us by legitimizing some of our conceptions, so that we believe they are the absolute truth.

The first coaching session: objectives and framework

At the first coaching session the coach and client must decide what the shared process should focus on. The coach must make clear what roles the coach and client are going to play, and how they will work through the process.

It is important to keep the "field" open, so that the angle of approach and ambience are open and investigative. Important areas might be overlooked otherwise. In the first session the goals and framework of the coaching have to be fixed. This means that the focus must be set at this stage. A fairly limited area is to be examined in the coming sessions: what is it; what is relevant to the goal? It is obvious that a coach's thorough professionalism cannot succeed on its own. Experience can prove to be a trap if it stands alone. But both systematized experience and personal (emotional and intuitive) experience, when contained by professionalism, are desirable and necessary factors.

With regard to framework and role, the coach must make the following clear to the client.

- Coaching is a joint process, where the efforts of both are crucial. The client must be ready to open up and talk honestly about the events in question. No developments can come from deliberate attempts to hide, embellish, or make up reality, or from excluding it and making it worse than it is. The client must try to open up in the face of whatever associations and emotions appear in the course of the work, consider them as data, and describe them in the session. In short, the client must make an effort to come in contact with him/herself.
- The coach must become involved in the work and put forward possible hypotheses, and let the client know what relevant ideas and possible explanations turn up in the coach's impressions. The coach will help to bring data forward by means of questions, structuring, assignments, and so on. The coach's hypotheses and interpretations will be based on a combination of experience, data from what the client tells him/her, including the client's associations and the like, and data from "inside" the coach. The coach will practise according to his/her knowledge and training, and according to the situation and the goal of the coaching.
- If there are any disturbances with regard to what is described above, it must, as far as possible, be brought up in the session, since that, too, will be valuable and useful data. This applies to both client and coach.

The coach will fill in a worksheet (see Appendix 2) with important information about the client. The goal for the coaching will also be written on this worksheet, so it must be defined in words at the first session. It might be something that can be done quickly, or it might require a little more time, or perhaps it will turn out to be part of the development process in itself. It might be the subject that takes up the whole of the first session.

Karen: case continued

Karen arrives too early for her first session. She apologises, and then adds quickly, "That sort of thing happens, after all. There are those days when you really ought to get more done than is possible. And you are so afraid of coming late, so you end up coming too early! Well, I suppose we have to make a start? Where are we going to talk?" She looks about her. Karen is older than I expected—forty-five, as it turns out. She appears more or less as I had imagined: not so tall, slender, modern, well dressed, and with an accommodating expression on her face. We settle ourselves in the study, sitting opposite each other with a small table between us. Karen's chair is a comfortable armchair that can be tipped back to a lying-down position. My chair is a slightly less soft armchair that lets me assume a good, upright sitting position. I ask her to put into words what she wants to be able to do when the coaching is over. She answers quickly, "I would like to be a little more 'tough'—isn't that what it is called? I want to have finished my work mentally when I come home. It is no use that I am so emotionally involved with the difficulties at work."

*　*　*

During this first session, it is important that the coach concentrates on establishing the relationship and is aware of everything that is happening here-and-now, while, at the same time, she is attending to projections from the client and how to tackle them as the coach, and whatever else is aroused inside the coach. Focus on the client, on oneself in the role of the coach, and on what is "in between". The coach must make use of empathy, create nearness and emotional contact with the client and what she says, without forgetting the "detective work". This means showing genuine curiosity in collecting data. Why is this matter so important to the client, so important that she both wants and feels a need to spend time and money on it? How did things get "this far"? In the example with Karen, what has prevented her from having the degree of "toughness" she wants? I wonder if she knows herself, or knows what could possibly be the reason. If she wants to be "tough", does she mean generally, or specifically in relation to some particular threat or threats? Has she worked at it before? Is it a new desire and need, or one she knows already?

It is important to be present emotionally. A technically perfect coach who poses the "right" wise questions, but is not emotionally present will have difficulty in establishing the relationship that is crucial if the client is to achieve self-development.

Case (continued)

It turns out that Karen is alone with a son who is autistic. He attends a special school and is, therefore, looked after in a care scheme connected with the school. Karen has set up an agreement herself with his learning support assistant, who brings the son home and stays with him there until Karen comes home. This is a private arrangement, outside the established system. Karen describes her situation informatively and neutrally. She would like to be a hundred per cent present when she is at home, and this has not been possible for her recently, since she has been responsible for carrying out a restructuring of the organization. Her thoughts have been busy working out how to arrange interviews with colleagues, how they would react, and afraid that they might start crying, worrying that they might be angry, or go on sick leave, and wondering how to explain to each one why it was her and not someone else who was being moved, and so on. It had taken up her attention to an uncomfortable degree: she became absent-minded, let the food burn on the stove, forgot to go to exercise sessions with her son, and was despondent, made excuses for not going to dinner with friends, and woke up sweating at night. She thought if she could not be more cool and collected, then she was not suited to her job as a leader, so it would be better to hand in her notice, find another job, and get away from it all. In the mornings things took on more reasonable proportions as a rule, but she still found it a burden. She cancelled relief weekends for her son because she felt guilty about not being a proper mother, with the result that she was completely run down and beginning to lose weight. She had not seen a doctor. "After all, I'm not ill," and she added, "Well, I suppose there could be something wrong with my soul," in a very quiet voice.

Karen had a previous job in leadership, which was very demanding, but also very interesting. She liked her work very much, but did not feel she performed satisfactorily in the earlier job. That was why she asked to be transferred to another area. "And then one has to take the consequences oneself. It should not make trouble for anyone else."

She is highly valued at work, and people are willing to co-operate with her. Everything went quietly and smoothly until this restructuring process, in which the secretariat was to be reduced by almost half the number of employees. No one was to be dismissed, but they were to be transferred to other areas. While Karen told me this, she was clearly coming into contact with many of the emotions that had been felt on the way through the process. She cries, but tries to hold it back. She apologizes that she is so soft, and is clearly ill at ease crying in someone else's presence. Karen emphasizes several times that it is herself that in some way is not "made of the right stuff", and that is why she cannot cope, even though she tries with all her might. To my question about what "the right stuff" is, she answers: "Well, something like having the right character, not having too many faults."

As mentioned in connection with Karen's first enquiry, it might be relevant to make a start in several of the fields illustrated in Figure 1. The first session must, therefore, reveal where the starting point is to be. Which is the first field to be investigated more thoroughly? The fact that one starts with a particular focus does not bar the coach's attention from the other fields at the same time. Organizational and group psychology are not excluded, but are still there in the background, just like role and couple psychology. In the example with Karen, several things indicate that it might be wise to start with her personal story: for one thing, there is a lot of data showing that Karen herself finds it relevant to search there. She imagines that the solution might be in strengthening herself, that something in her should be reinforced or established, being more cool and tough, not having so many weaknesses, being "made of the right stuff", etc. One could also point out the absence of any conception (or at least any formulated conception) that her difficult situation could have anything to do with "the others"—disadvantages in life—or anything else that pointed away from herself. There are many data, too, indicating that Karen is a person who is very concerned about moral values, and there are many normative statements. Karen takes it on her own shoulders when something does not function properly: looking for a different job because she feels she is inadequate in the face of demands, she cannot fill the position completely. She does not ask herself whether it could be the demands, the situation, or the terms of the job that were unreasonable. The situations where Karen is moved emotionally and where she loses control are when she talks about situations where she feels she has failed. From a psychological point of view, this could mean both when she has let someone down, or when someone else has let her down.

I share some of my observations with Karen, and give reasons for my choice of starting point. I tell her that when one is working psychodynamically, one of the fundamental hypotheses is that nothing happens by chance, and that we have to understand the events in our lives as interconnected. (This is known in the theory as psychological determinism: that in the mind, just as in the physical world, nothing happens by chance, and every psychological event is determined by what has gone before (Brenner, 1984).) When something becomes too oppressive and disruptive, it is necessary to investigate how it relates to earlier events in life. So, our joint task in the next coaching sessions will be to investigate in *what way* the present situation is connected with her earlier life. Thus, Karen's task will be to begin telling her personal story. My role will be to support and act as a catalyst for Karen's active efforts to understand her inner psychological logic.

Karen and I agree to reserve the time for ten two-hour sessions for the process. It is the coach's task to manage the physical setting and the time framework, beginning punctually, ending on time, structuring the time, and managing the sub-tasks along the way. It might be wise to point out shortly before the end of a session that there are ten or fifteen minutes left. This allows the client, who may be in the middle of something involving emotions, a chance to "unwind" before the session ends. When the session is over, the client should be able to accommodate everything him/herself. It is also the coach's responsibility to draw attention to the point in the process where the current session is. This could be at the beginning or the end of the session. It is particularly important to draw attention to the fact when the end of a course is approaching. This makes it possible to work on a parting theme in connection with the relationship that has been "at work" in the coaching, and must now end.

Along the way, it is also the coach's responsibility to sum up how far the work has progressed in relation to the goal. The goal in the example is that Karen must have a basic and certain sense of having become stronger as a person. This new strength must manifest itself as greater self-satisfaction and joy of life. At the practical level, this new strength must help in enabling Karen to structure both her working life and her everyday life so that it is less wearing, and allows room for more of the events that give renewed energy and enjoyment. Thus, it is a goal where she wants something added and something eliminated. The goal and the framework are the result of a joint effort, and are written down. The coach can, for instance, ask the client the following questions when the time to end the session is approaching, but not so late that there is not enough time to answer and work on the answer. "If we think of the goal for this coaching, what point have you reached in relation to it? Are you closer? Are things going the right way? In what ways are you closer or further away?" If the answer is that the client thinks we are a long way from the goal, it is natural to follow up by asking how and why—in the client's view— we have moved away from the goal. In this way it is possible to place the client and oneself in a metaposition in relation to the coaching, and process–evaluate the content and the relationship.

The course of coaching

In Karen's case, the first session had been held and there were now nine sessions remaining for the rest of the process, of which the last would be for rounding off. If Karen wished to continue after that, we would not make any decision about it until after this course of coaching had ended. This principle is useful, because a moderate, reasonable pressure of time helps to keep things in focus. We both know that there is something we have to do within an agreed time limit, which means Karen has to make an effort to be attentive, honest, and open, and I must offer interpretations and actions that deliberately work on her defences.

Case (continued)

Karen arrives eight minutes late for the next session. I make use of my worksheet (see Appendix 3) to note down what is happening. In the right-hand column I write: Is the delay resistance to getting started on this task? Then I ask Karen, "What are your thoughts and feelings at the beginning of this task?" Karen tells me that she both wants to be here, get started, and be free from the "heavy problems", but she also feels like leaving; she does not want to make contact with her story. I note that she is aware of her ambivalence, an ambivalence that may extend far beyond starting this task. It was, in any case, something I had noticed intuitively from the beginning. She had had a dream, and told me about it. I asked her to explain how she understood it herself, the meanings of the various animals, people, and things or symbols that appear in it. What emotions are there in the various relationships? I note in my right-hand column that Karen is "a good dreamer". I contribute my interpretation of the dream in an enquiring tone; in other words, as hypotheses and questions that can be confirmed or rejected. When I work through the session afterwards, I become aware that I have a positive countertransference associated with clients who dream. I find dreams very interesting as data. Professionally, I also enjoy the richness often found in dreams. They are also entertaining. So, I end up transmitting a signal that the client is "clever" or "interesting", and this disturbs the transference relationship.

* * *

Taking the personal story as the starting point (that is, in the field of personality and developmental psychology) does not mean that the present is kept out of sight. Dreams are material that gives information about the present state of the inner process. In traditional psychoanalysis, the dream is considered as the "royal road to the unconscious" (Freud, 1915e). It is founded on the way that "behind every dream is active unconscious thinking" (Brenner, 1984, p. 17), and "The study of dreams leads especially to the mental content that has been repressed or by some other means excluded from consciousness and expatiation as a result of the Ego's defence activities" (Brenner, 1984, p. 127). The interpretation of material from dreams can, therefore, be very informative in the process that goes on in psychodynamic coaching, both in relation to the point the client has reached in the current development process and in relation to repressed material. As a coach, it is easy to be pleased when one's client proves to be " a good dreamer". However, if being pleased in this way becomes too obvious in the transference–countertransference balance, so that the client consciously or unconsciously "catches" it, the wish to be a good and/or interesting client might lead the client to increase the production of dreams by means of letting the accounts become all-important, and the actual, focused work of coaching might be side-tracked. In short, an new form of defence (Tähkä, 1983). As a rule, residues from the day also appear in dreams: these are elements of daily life that can also provide data about connections between present and past. It will also be natural to allow a place for everyday situations that are relevant to the coaching, since the overall goal of the coaching is to free the client from dilemmas that come up in present everyday life precisely by investigating the connections between past and present.

The subsequent coaching sessions will pursue exactly this overriding question: which connections are there between the client's personal story and the present situation? There are many ways to begin work on the personal story. The coach can take a more or less active part in structuring the way it is approached The most unstructured way, with the least control, is to ask the client to tell his/her personal story, and choose the starting point and course of events. The coach takes up a listening position, in which it is possible to intervene and take notes while listening. There are different opinions about a coach making notes as the story is told. One opinion is that it is disturbing for both parties, shifts the focus, and signals a lack of attentiveness, and that it is superfluous, because what needs to be remembered will be remembered, if one listens properly and attentively. Another opinion is that it fixes elements that one would not, in fact, be able to remember, because of one's own suppressions, especially factors connected with countertransference: the emotions, thoughts, and associations that arise inside the coach along the way. My approach lies somewhere between these two: to make notes discreetly. That means not all the time, and providing it does not disturb the situation, and, in fact, supports it instead. This is really one of the factors—in my practice—where a therapy situation is different from a coaching situation. It highlights the active and joint nature of the work. What I note down can be used directly in the process.

The account of the personal story can also begin with a drawing. The coach could, for instance, give the client the following assignment: "Draw seven events from your life, and at least two must be from your childhood." The possibilities in a drawing are different from those in a verbal opening. There is a shared third item that can be observed, which might be stimulating for the work done and for freedom to "talk about". Drawings include a lot of unconscious material to work on, and can serve as leads to associations, which may prove very advantageous.

There are other ways of structuring the work, such as asking the client to describe situations and relationships with the help of metaphors, or one can select periods or themes. One can work by acting through scenes. In this method, the client and coach together design scenes like the original one and assign roles such as a conversation between a mother and child, for instance. The client, as the person who knows the story, is the instructor, and in this way particular scenes can be created, altered, and played again. The two can exchange roles to investigate different positions and states of mind, adjustments can be made and the scene repeated, etc. It is important that the client considers the situations as essential, representative, and meaningful. Situations like that often contain a great deal of information about what characterizes the chosen relationship—in this case between mother and child. When the situation has been played through, the subsequent discussion and examination is crucial, as this is where the detective work goes on. The discussion might lead to the scene or situation being acted through once more. Setting up a scene makes it possible to work very thoroughly through it. This method also makes it possible to play out the "desired" version, or other variations of the same situation. This means it is possible to work on forming the future and, in that way, discover at the emotional level how it *could* be. This expands the repertory, and the psychodynamics between the play of conscious and unconscious forces are loosened. Setting up a scene, as in the method I have described here, is inspired by psychodrama (Blatner, 1996) and drama therapy (Jennings, 1992). It is important to ensure that the opening moves in coaching are well thought out with regard to the client and the client's goal, since it has a determining status in connection with the entire process.

In practical terms, it is a good idea for the client and coach to sit so that they can both see each other, or not look at each other, without this feeling awkward or unfriendly. There must be freedom allowing for both, while at the same time the coach must be able to observe the client without the client feeling too much like an exhibit on display. A setting where the client and coach sit beside each other, slightly at an angle to each other, perhaps with a small table between them, will make this possible. If the client's chair can also be tipped to a half-reclining position, it gives the client maximum freedom. One could also choose the more traditional setting for psychoanalysis, with the client lying on a couch and the coach sitting in a chair that is comfortable, but still clearly a working chair. This will undeniably be associated with therapy, and does not emphasize so effectively that the process going on is coaching.

Case (continued)

I asked Karen to tell me her story. Chronologically, with special emphasis on situations and relationships she remembered especially clearly, and on the feelings and conceptions she had had in those periods. Karen was willing to do that, but said it was difficult, because there is so much she could not remember, so it would be very subjective. What if it showed everything in a worse light than it should, or gave a misleading impression—then it would be untrue, so would it really help? "After all, I had a happy childhood and good parents." Understandably, Karen was afraid of taking a firm hold of her story. What underlying reasons could there be? What will show up for me? Imagine, if I am manipulated and lured into a worse situation than the one I am in now? These are thoughts that might come to her. I noted (Appendix 3) "defence against fear". I asked Karen: "What other thoughts and feelings do you have associated with what you are about to look into now?" "Well, I might be unjust to someone, and that is not fair." "Who might you be unjust to?" "Well, I am thinking most about my father and mother." "I can quite understand that you do not want to be unjust to anyone. What would it mean to you, if it happened in relation to your father and mother?" I noted on my worksheet (Appendix 3) that she says father before mother. Karen was silent. For five minutes. It seemed a long time in this situation. Karen was in tears, sniffed, looked a little irritated, and said, "Well, you shouldn't do it. It's not right, and it would reflect back on me." "Where did you learn that?" "That's just how it is," she replied at once. I could sense the annoyance and coldness directed at me. If I brought the feelings in this situation up to the surface I could read between the lines that I was supposed to retreat, because I was facing a higher force. "That's just how it is," Karen answered firmly, as if it was one of the laws of nature or something equivalent. It was my impression that Karen had often met that kind of higher force, and it could almost be felt as if her superego was talking to her id (me). Or that she was reproducing what she knew best—she was responding to others as they responded to her. I said, "That is how it feels to you right now. It doesn't feel like that to me. Perhaps that is one of the things that it is important to look into more carefully, which truths you are carrying with you about 'the way it is', and what it means to you." I continued, "We have set up a goal for the task we are going to carry out here. That might mean that you run the risk—or I would say you can't avoid it—of saying something subjective, or something you have experienced personally, and something that might be unfair to someone or something, because everything we feel or experience is subjective. We are subjects, and none of us knows what is true. You have come because you want to develop. Developing yourself will involve difficult feelings of frustration, pain, and anger. But it also leads to greater freedom. Now, we are working together, so there are two of us to understand and bear it." Karen looked at me, listening seriously like a child, then nodded and began her story.

* * *

The example above shows how the relationship develops. If coaching is to work, a relationship has to be built up that will allow transference from the client to the coach. Precisely this kind of situation is characteristic for the association with the psychodynamic tradition, and is, therefore, a distinguishing characteristic of psychodynamic coaching: that the relationship between the client and the coach is the central medium through which the psychological change takes place. The account above also shows how countertransference is used in this work. Countertransference is seen as a kind of advanced empathy, or a high degree of mentalization, which makes it possible to understand the unconscious dynamics that are transferred from the client. The coach must assume a psychological position that corresponds to the parents' position, so that the original relationships and their significance can be cancelled and replaced by something more mature.

Case (continued)

Karen "falls into line" and begins her story. What follows is a condensed version of Karen's story. She came from the south west of Jutland in Denmark. She was an only child, and her parents were relatively old when she was born. The home was deeply Christian, as members of the revivalist Inner Mission in Denmark. Karen was brought up to say grace before meals and go to Sunday School. Her parents were immeasurably glad finally to have been "given" a child after many years of involuntary childlessness. "Given" was understood as "given by God". There was an undertone suggesting that a boy would have been better, but, since things could not be changed, they were fine as they were. Karen's mother came from a family with higher social status than the father's family. Karen's maternal grandfather was a minister of an independent church, and was very highly thought of and respected in the local community. Her father started out as a smallholder with his own cottage and smallholding, but things did not go very well. The larger, mechanized farms managed better, and kept down the prices of agricultural produce. The smallholders could not make a living, and Karen's father sold the land, although they went on living in the house. Her father worked for the post office, and her mother was a housewife at home.

The mother had ambitions for Karen, and wanted her to go to high school and then to a teacher training college. Karen spent a lot of time on her schoolwork. She attended Sunday School until the third form, and in her free time took part in club work at church. Her friends were from the same church environment. She worked very hard, and did well at school, especially at mathematics. Karen went on to high school, which was in a larger town, and meant a lot of time spent travelling to and fro. She did not know her new classmates, and they came from completely different backgrounds from Karen. She was considered rather a swot, but survived on friendly terms with the group because the others could borrow her physics reports and maths homework to help them write their own.

Karen was lonely, but made friends with Søren, a boy of the same age who was in the parallel class. Søren was a bright student, and did well with very little effort. He was slightly freaky, smoked hash, and was an active member of the Communist Youth of Denmark movement. Karen was fascinated by Søren, his eloquence, his social-mindedness, and everything that was so different about him and the background he came from. She did not say anything about Søren at home. In connection with a school party during the second year, Karen asked permission to stay the night with one of the other girls. In fact, she slept with Søren in the commune where he lived. She became pregnant, and did not dare to tell her parents. She did not tell Søren either. Instead, she ran away from home and sought refuge with a maths teacher with whom she felt secure. The maths teacher got in touch with Karen's parents, who came and took her home. She told them she was pregnant, but not who the father was. Her parents were deeply shocked, scolded her and reproached her, saying she lived like a hussy, and asking whether she had any thought for them. They had scrimped and scraped to give her a better start than they had had themselves, and so on. It was a scandal that would brand them as bad parents in church circles and in the local community. Later, it clouded their lives and they reproached themselves: they had not taken good enough care of Karen, and this illegitimate baby was God's punishment.

Karen had to leave school, and was sent to live with an aunt, her father's sister, who lived in Djursland, on the eastern side of Jutland. The aunt was unmarried, and a Christian nursing sister at a nursing home. Karen was informed by her aunt, when the time to give birth was approaching, that the aunt and Karen's parents thought the baby should be given away for adoption. That would be best for the baby, and best for Karen, who could continue her studies and then get married properly. "Once it is all sorted out, you will forget about it." Karen was devastated, and seemed to fall into a black hole. The baby was given away for adoption, and Karen was sent to a boarding school run by the Inner Mission to complete the third year of high school. She could remember very little about the final year of high school, except that she seemed to have homework all the time, and dreamed of running away from it all as soon as she had finished the course. She passed her high school exams, the "studentereksamen", and, at the age of eighteen, set off to Copenhagen. She had decided that she would have nothing more to do with her parents. She intended to forget all about her childhood and Jutland.

She enrolled to study politics at university, found a room in a hall of residence, and generally lived the life of a student. During the first years she went to a lot of parties and did not think about the future. Then she met a fellow student called Ole, and they became lovers. They moved into a flat together, completed their studies, and both found good jobs in government offices. They had some crises, partly because they had problems with their sex life. Karen did not feel really feminine—she described it as largely neuter. Her relationship with Ole was more like a friendship or the relationship of a brother and sister than lovers. Karen was terrified of getting pregnant, and had never told Ole her story about the baby that was adopted. "It was as if it had never happened—I had forgotten all about it too." They put all their energy into their careers. They spent a lot of time seeing friends, who were either former fellow students or new colleagues, but as their friends had children and moved out of town, they had less and less in common. Ole wanted to have children, and Karen tried to delay it. She succeeded in this for several years, but finally became pregnant. When Karen had the baby, he turned out to be "different", but there did not seem to be any diagnosis. Karen took leave from work to be with the baby full time. The relationship between Karen and Ole was getting worse. Karen had very dark moods and started to think it must be God's punishment because she had failed her first baby. She was referred to a psychiatrist, who diagnosed her as depressive and prescribed medicine and a course of therapy sessions. It helped, and she went back to her job. Karen and Ole got help with their son, who proved to be autistic. The two of them slipped away from each other, and then Ole found a new partner, so he wanted a divorce. "It was almost a relief. Then there was only one of them for me to look after."

Gradually, Karen got her life under control with her son. She asked for a different, less demanding job, and organized school, a care institution, and a relief place for her son. Her courage returned as she felt her ability to manage all this alone, and, at the same time, she discovered many of the pleasures of being a mother. Karen promised herself that she would never again let herself be dependent on anyone. "No one was ever going to rule over my life again." She did not think much about the child she had given away for adoption or of her childhood. That chapter was closed, and could not be changed, so it was no use dwelling on the past. "Every time I think about it, I let my son down. So I have put it behind me for ever." Karen told me how well things functioned in her daily life, how efficient and well organized she had become, "So there was time for the really important things." Right until she had to implement this reorganization.

*   *   *

Some people's lives conceal more dramatic—or at least different—stories from what one would imagine. Stories with many strong feelings attached that the client has learnt to suppress, because they were too illegitimate, or difficult, or perhaps threatening. Feelings the client has not really been in contact with, and, therefore, has not really managed to investigate and come to terms with them or accommodate them unaided. It is important that the coach can tolerate hearing the story without being overwhelmed or frightened, without wanting to react from feelings of countertransference and express them, or whatever else can arise regarding antipathy and sympathy as the story is told. The coach must be able to *contain* it all, keep focused on the task, and work sensitively, with human engagement, but professionally, free of values, throughout the whole course.

The concept of containing was developed by Bion (1961), and described, originally, a mother's capacity to receive the feelings the child cannot accommodate him/herself, and to process them and return them to the child so that it is possible for the child to accommodate them. In coaching, it means the coach's ability to accommodate the client's feelings and narrative, which involves not reacting to fend them off, but specifically listening to them, joining the client in them, and, thus, processing them in such a way that the client does not need to flee from them (again), but can stay in them without being bowled over by fear. One could say that it is the coach's ability to render down the difficult things, so that they can be used constructively again, rather like composting.

The ability to contain belongs, to some extent, together with another concept, that of creating a "holding environment", a considerate environment. The coach's ability to create a considerate environment is crucial to coaching. A considerate environment is where both the physical and the psychological surroundings have been taken into consideration. The physical surroundings have already been described, such as the setting and the time frame. However, they also include the furnishings of the room where the coaching takes place. They must be suitably neutral, so that they influence the client as little as possible. They must not, therefore, be full of the coach's personal items. It is also part of the considerate environment that the coaching happens in the same place every time, and that there cannot be any interruptions. Sounds must not carry through the building, and there must not be too much noise. Finally, another important factor for feeling secure is that the coach should feel comfortable in the room and be good at emanating the fact. When the coach feels sure that he/she can accommodate whatever might come, it fills the room. When the client senses the coach's containing capacity during the process, it stimulates what is safe and secure in the process.

In Karen's story there are many difficult feelings and fantasies about connections that are almost unbearable. However, she has found a balance, or equilibrium, where her life works. Nevertheless, this balance is delicate, because it is founded on repressions, pain, pent-up anger, and despair. Karen has succeeded in fitting together the jigsaw of her life and her son's through fantastic strength of will. On the way through Karen's story, feelings and memories turn up that surprise her, because she thought those chapters were closed. Heavy feelings of shame and guilt weigh down her understanding of why her life has taken the course that it has. We came a long way in the coaching process before the interaction between then and now became clear to Karen. The balance she had managed to establish in her life toppled when she was asked to move people against their will. It was her superiors who had asked her to do this. Karen is extremely loyal and conscientious about her tasks and her workplace, precisely as she had been as a child with her parents. It does not occur to her that she might question the authorities' values. When she can see that she cannot carry out a task and get top marks for it, she assumes the responsibility and asks to be transferred to another job. Her otherwise highly realistic abilities are disengaged. When Karen explained about the reasons why her father had to sell his smallholding, she was surprised at her own detailed understanding of the situation. She could remember listening very carefully when her father talked about it, and she understood that everything to do with economy was really serious, and that it was almost the end of the world for anyone who was not able to manage independently. In the middle of her narrative she exclaimed, "But that is why I became an economist. Just think—I had never thought of it before!"

Today, she is the leader of a secretariat that deals with public welfare. When Karen talked about the colleagues she had to transfer, she discovered that she was full of the same feelings as in the situation with the baby she had to give away for adoption. First she did it, almost without feeling, and without asking anyone for help or advice, blindly obedient. Afterwards, she was overwhelmed by a feeling of guilt about getting pregnant, and then letting her baby down by giving it away. This is mixed with endless pain and feelings of emptiness and loss. The loss relates both to the baby that was given away and to herself; to what, deep inside, she had wanted and not had from her parents all her life. When Karen realized this, she was furious with her parents, and regained some of the energy she had had in the relationship with Søren and the incipient rebellion in the relationship. She compared her own feelings for her son with her experience of what her mother had felt for her. She could not understand how her mother could have been so unfeeling. "But I don't know her story either. Her childhood home was not exactly characterized by anything but darkness and condemnation."

At this point in the process, Karen came into contact with the Inner Mission as she had known it as a child, and which she thought she had broken away from and finished with when she cancelled her membership of the church. However, it became clear to her that she still carried with her the fancy that her son's autism was God's punishment for getting pregnant in sin and then giving her baby away for adoption. Karen was embarrassed and mortified when she discovered this. But when she caught sight of it, she could see, at the same time, that her mother's action had been "illogical": it was, after all, her mother's decision that the baby should be adopted. Thus, the first sin—getting pregnant—was Karen's, but the next sin, giving the baby away, was her mother's, and not Karen's at all. Was it for the sake of her reputation in the local community? Or was it to punish Karen? Or because she was envious at the way Karen got pregnant so easily, when she herself had found it so difficult? It was possible to see her mother as complicit, because she had come to terms with many of her feelings, and in that way it became possible to wonder, to question some of the explanations that previously had been so unequivocal. There was room to allow an essential part of Karen's identity, that of being a rational, logically thinking person, to be applied to her own life. Suddenly, several of the things she had understood before did not seem logical. There was something that did not tally. It opened up possibilities for looking more soberly and maturely at the management's demand that she should implement the most difficult part of the change in the organization—moving loyal older colleagues. What had they "landed" on her? Was it reasonable? Could she not have insisted that it would be more logical if they—who had made the decision—took that action themselves?

At the last but one session I reminded Karen that the next session was the last, and our task would be to look back at the goal, and evaluate the process and our relationship. Until then, each session had been more or less structured in this way: introduction (5–10 minutes); present situation (15–20 minutes); "detective work" (about an hour); reflection (20–30 minutes).

Case (continued)

I said, "Good afternoon, Karen, this is the nth session. And the goal with our work is that you should have an underlying secure feeling that you have become stronger as a person. This new strength must manifest itself as greater self-satisfaction and pleasure in your life. You must be able to use this new strength to structure both your working life and your everyday life so that it is less wearing, frustrating, and allows room for more of the events that give renewed energy and enjoyment. How are we getting on with it in general?"

Fifteen to twenty minutes' discussion ensued about the present situation, and what had happened since last time with regard to the goal. It took the form of a sort of investigative and informational interview.

At a suitable transition, I said, "We must go a bit further with our work. Last time you were busy with . . ." And then, with the support of my notes (Appendix 3), I mentioned the main points that Karen had talked about last time. "What I have been thinking about since last time is this . . ." And again I looked at my notes (Appendix 3). At this stage, I contribute any of my thoughts, hypotheses, and associations that I consider will act as catalysts in the process. Here, I can introduce my countertransferences, where, for instance, a hypothesis might have arisen from a sensation of countertransference. In this way, I provide new data in the coaching process. When it was Karen's turn to comment, she was asked to give her views of what I said.

Karen continued working by reflecting on the data she had received from me. After that she continued her story, which was primarily a monologue, but with occasional interventions from me. These could be supplementary, or could be confrontations or interpretations.

About thirty minutes before our time was up, I observed that we had half an hour of the session left. Jointly, we reflected on, and associated with, what had been told. In this part of the interview we also draw in the feelings that have arisen in our relationship along the way.

When there was no more time, I drew attention to that, and we said goodbye.

Conclusion: evaluation and leave-taking

There are two objectives in the last session: to evaluate, reflect over, and conclude the process, and to close the relationship.

Case (continued)

Karen and I looked again at the goal. Had it been achieved? Karen wanted to be more "tough", and that was "translated" as: Karen should have a basic and certain sense of having become stronger as a person. This new strength must manifest itself as greater self-satisfaction and joy of life. At the practical level, this new strength must help to enable Karen to structure both her working life and her everyday life so that it is less wearing, and allows room for more of the events that give renewed energy and enjoyment.

When it was Karen's turn to talk, she was surprised that she felt more certain of herself, freer, but it was very different from what she had expected. She felt more sensitive and frail, "But now I know where it is, I think I won't be so surprised." She mentioned the specific steps she had taken about the organization of her life. She had created more space for herself with a clear conscience. She was considering finding a new job, following her ambition of "going a bit further", and had already seen a possibility. This last matter was something she might come back to in a new process. The last thing Karen mentioned, blushing, was that it was not exactly impossible that she could imagine herself finding a partner at some time. "I don't want to be alone all my life." About our relationship, she told me that she had at times been so furious with me that she wanted to drop the whole project. "I got the impression that you were sitting there with all the answers, and just wanted to roast me over a slow fire until I found them myself. But I found out that you were not my mother, and that you were not at all tight-fisted about sharing your observations with me, so that I could find them myself and decide what I wanted."

We parted, and it is really sad when a relationship that has been meaningful comes to an end. It is also sad for the coach. But it is not unbearable. The parting is the platform where something else begins, something new, with new initiatives and new processes. This applies to both client and coach.

*   *   *

The case with Karen started out from her personal story. The "risk" in this starting point—quite contrary to the idea of psychodynamic coaching—is that focus will centre on the individual alone. There is a risk that the problems will be individualized, and the system, its psychodynamics, and their interaction with the individual disappear from the field. When a coaching process starts out from this field, it is crucial that the coach must be aware of the system perspective all the time. In Karen's case, there were many systems that were involved along the way. The church environment of her childhood was a system with very closed boundaries and a simplified main purpose. The exchanges across the boundaries, that is, communications and inter-play between someone inside the system and someone outside, were minimal, and there is a high risk in a system like that of unhealthy developments. The individual, in this case Karen, becomes entwined in the dynamics, and it can be almost impossible to untangle oneself, or imagine contact with anyone outside, without it then becoming a categorical break with the system. When Karen decided to go to Copenhagen, she did break off contact with her parents, synonymous with the system, for always. The logic of the system is a paranoid–schizoid logic: black or white, true or false, good or evil, the faithful and the unbelievers, saved or lost souls.[1] Karen was swallowed up or infected by this logic, and took it with her, even though she believed she had broken away from the system of her childhood. This was one of the liberating discoveries Karen made in the process. It was liber-ating because it opened up the possibility of working on it again, and thus in reality making oneself freer. The discovery that everything was not connected with her, so that she was the problem, suddenly made other, multi-faceted explanations and forms of logic possible. In the organisation where she worked, there were also special forms of dynamics between the senior management and the employees. When they interacted with the system-bound forms of logic Karen had learnt at home, the result was that she took over the responsibility for deal-ing with "the bad side" on behalf of the senior management. The management wanted to project this "bad side" away from themselves, and Karen had an unconscious agenda, in which she had to atone for her sin. This built a non-constructive collusion between Karen and the system.[2] It is the responsibility of the coach to draw the system into perspective when the personal and individual aspects take up too much attention. Similarly, it is the coach's responsibility to draw in the individual aspect when the system perspective takes up too much attention. The process Karen went through may seem like therapy. It was not therapy, and the objective is not to examine the client's underlying problem and bring healing. Karen was not ill. The frequency and duration were not the same as in a therapeutic course of treatment. My role and interaction with Karen were far from therapy, and above all, that was not what Karen had asked for. She had asked for help to deal with a specific situation, and that was what she got. Coaching has a specific goal, and the work moves deliberately towards it. Karen's story is not exactly ordinary, so there are many elements in her personal story. Anyone who has heard many people's stories will know that there are more unusual stories than ordinary ones. We tend to imagine otherwise, because often we do not tell our stories to each other either. Most people's stories are novels. In Karen's case, however, there is no doubt that the coaching clearly had a therapeutic effect. That is one of the "risks" of working seriously with one's personal development.

Notes

1. Paranoid–schizoid is a concept that originates from Melanie Klein's theory of development. It describes a position in infants where the world of experience is characterized by persecution and splitting. It is a state that arises in the attempt to soothe the anxiety that occurs in the child when the reality of the fact that good and evil are linked is acknowledged. This is explained in more detail in the chapter about personality and developmental psychology.
2. Collusion is a mutual process, where a sender transmits projections to a receiver, who in turn identifies with them: that is, absorbs them and "becomes" the projection.

CHAPTER THREE

Individual psychodynamic coaching

We are conceived, and we emerge from our mothers into the world. Each of us is "someone" from the start of life. We consist of a number of biological possibilities and limitations. We meet the world on the outside. It is a world that partly determines who we will become. The environment inside our mothers has—in all probability—already played its part. Our personalities are forming. Personality is a central concept when we describe and comprehend a person. It is vital in psychodynamic coaching to understand—or comprehend—the client as an individual, as a person and as an entity. Understanding how personality is formed is an essential part of the background knowledge that coaching is based on. It is essential because people always have their childhood with them as a sounding board for later experiences and actions. The coach needs to take into serious consideration *who* it is who is sitting opposite him or her. One must not take a fixed or diagnostic view, but look in a way that embraces and attempts to accommodate the complexity comprised in the other person. There must be respect for the fact that the other person never can be completely understood, so the coach's approach must be open and allow space. Experience can be both a help and an impediment. Experience can result in blindness to some of the facts, but also brings sense (or, rather, wisdom, which I define as experienced and repeated knowledge, experience-based evidence), so that the client is relatively quickly identified and "recognized" by the coach.

An understanding of the client as an individual is not something that has to be "seen to" at the beginning, or needs to be "in place" before the work can begin. It is a continuing process that goes on in parallel with the coaching. It makes a coaching process secure and effective. It means security for the client, because it keeps the individual aspect in view: the client is regarded as a whole, not in fragments, and not only as part of a system. Just because the client comes to coaching with a wish for change, the client must not be identified with this reason alone for coming, but also with everything else that the client also is. The right understanding of the client imparts effectiveness, because an experienced coach in particular will have seen and heard many things, and does not need to relate to any surprises at an individual level. Experience is to be understood as having both systematized and non-systematized experiences and knowledge of possible connections between surface and depth, between the form of manifestation and the possible cause(s). This approach allows a wide scope for the interpretation of data and the ability and creativity to combine data in the process. In other words, this is an essential precondition for forming working hypotheses and possible interpretations along the way.

Personality involves the essence of a person (Carver & Scheier, 1992): that is, the lasting traits that characterize a person's actions and reactions, and are, to a certain degree, predictable (Gade, 2006). Many different schools of psychology offer their attempts to define the concept of personality. The domain of psychology is the healthy person, unlike the domain of somatic medicine, which is the diseased person. There are many different ways of being a healthy person. Nevertheless, a certain consensus is necessary about where the focus should be centred: which are the relevant markers, when we set out to describe the significant and important sides of someone's personality? The great majority of psychological schools of thought agree that personality is formed in the infant's interaction with its mother and the other immediate relationships. The relevant features relate to emotional makeup, and to social behaviour more than to cognitive abilities (Gade, 2006). According to Gade, there are, as yet, no data indicating that heredity is most significant in determining an individual's personality traits. However, it is agreed that biology—the structure of the brain—plays a central part. The underlying brain structure and its function are linked to experiences in the environment where the child grows up, during which the first four years are especially important (Gade, 2006). Hemmingsen and Rosenberg (1997) establish in a study that the following dimensions of personality are particularly important when we describe personality:

1. *Emotional stability*: the tendency towards emotional reactions and behaviour. Reduced stability increases the likelihood of anxiety, depression and anger.
2. *Impulsive stability*: the tendency to react impulsively in an unsocialized manner. A tendency to low stability will often mean difficulty in social relations with others.
3. *Social interaction*: the nature of relations with others—whether the person primarily seeks contact or avoids it.

These dimensions are determined by the brain structures that are formed in childhood. Not surprisingly, therefore, both biology and environment are significant in the formation of the underlying personality. Personality is not unalterable. It can be influenced and developed throughout life. The earliest-formed basic structures are extremely difficult to change, but corrections can be made in various ways. The psychoanalytical personality and development theories focus on the environment, especially on the early relationship between mother and child. Theories and empirically based knowledge have arisen in two ways: first by studying and analysing adults' accounts and memories of childhood, and later by studying childhood directly: for instance, by studying the interplay between mother and child. The personal history that is the foundation for personality is, therefore, relevant in connection with psychodynamic coaching. Personality is the concept we use when we talk about another person. Our own personality, as we experience it from inside ourselves, is designated by the concept of identity. Theories about which factors in early childhood are determinative, how, and in what way development is the co-designer of present possibilities, are, therefore, relevant both for someone who wants to get to know himself/herself, and for anyone concerned with psychodynamic coaching. As mentioned earlier, psychodynamic coaching also includes awareness that there is more than personality; there is "the third party"—the system—and the implicit external context. This might mean the family, partner, workplace, organization, group, assignment, association, etc. (Huffington, 2006). A person's current situation is always the result of an interplay between that person and the dynamics of the system. In order to understand a current situation and create possibilities for development, all three must be in focus: the person, the system, and the dynamic interplay. Below, I describe some central theories and concepts from psychodynamic theory that focus on personality and development, and how they become fundamental understandings in the work that is performed in psychodynamic coaching.

The psychoanalytical theories were developed one at a time, but inspired by each other, because a new approach is often triggered by an already existing theory. New approaches might be developed from an idea about further development, an idea about moderation because new data have appeared, or from an idea about abandoning one point of view in favour of another, but still within the same basic interpretation. These theories might well include mutual inconsistencies. The following summaries are far from complete: they are more like the minimum that is permissible. It is not my ambition to make this a psychodynamic reference work, but to give an overview of the diversity of the psychodynamic theories of personality and development. The reader is advised to seek more knowledge in the primary sources, that is, in the original works of the proponents of the theories.

Freud

The basic understanding of the psychodynamic approach was formulated by Freud, who perceived personality as consisting of three elements: the id, the ego and the superego. According to Freud, the id is the element of personality that the child has from birth. The other elements are formed gradually in the development process as the child grows older. According to Freud, personality is the means of managing the satisfaction of drives and needs and then the need for, and dependence on, social interaction (being in a social system). The id is controlled by the pleasure principle, which is the wish to gratify desires and avoid discomfort. The id consists of biological drives and impulses, and this element of the personality is unconscious. Freud believed that development was driven by urges: for instance, a child who feels hungry is experiencing a state of tension and, therefore, cries. In order to satisfy its hunger, a baby has to learn to restrain the driving impulse until its mother or the bottle is nearby. The baby's experience or inner remembered images of the breast or bottle that brings gratification will make it possible gradually to control the driving impulse. What happens within the baby based on the very first experiences is known as the primary process. Through these primary processes the child is enabled to relate to an increasing extent to the outside world. Freud calls this adaptation to reality. It leads to the development of the ego. The driving forces in the development of personality are the instinct for self-preservation and the sexual drive that arises in association with this instinct (Olsen, 2002; Olsen & Køppe, 1981). Two simultaneous, parallel, and interactive development processes take place, through which the child develops first the ego and then the superego: the adaptive development process and the psychosexual development process. The adaptive development is dependent on the instinct for self-preservation (also called self-assertion), which starts the development process, and which is then modified and supplemented by the psychosexual development, which is initiated by the sexual drive. The adaptive process is concerned with adaptation to the physical surroundings, and learning psychomotoric and cognitive skills. This adaptive development is divided into four phases (Olsen, 2002; Olsen & Køppe, 1981):

1. *The autoerotic:* when the bodily ego is formed. It is formed with the pleasure principle as its starting point.
2. *The narcissistic:* where the bodily ego is further developed to the pure pleasure ego, which is an ego completely devoid of distaste. It is preoccupied entirely with gratification. The child separates himself from everything distasteful by placing it outside himself. The child assimilates pleasurable elements outside its ego; for instance, the delight in its mother's attributes—breast and hands—and in that way the child feels omnipotent.
3. *The Oedipal:* where reality catches up with the child, and he has to find his bearings in relation to it, gathering experience through reality testing. The fantasy of omnipotence is redirected to the parents, who become the objects of idealization. The child

becomes the rival of the parent of the same sex as the child, trying to "win" the other parent.

4. *The post-Oedipal*: when the child experiences that it loses the struggle to push either its father or mother out of the way and take over that parent's place. This will be the last pervasive development of personality, as the superego is formed through internalization of the parent who is the same sex as the child. Thus, the superego acquires such a high degree of power that it controls the rest of the personality.

The psychosexual development falls similarly into four phases:

1. *The oral phase, from birth to two years*: the child's understanding of itself and its surroundings is via sensation through the mouth. The child perceives itself as connected symbiotically with its mother. The task of development in the oral phase could be expressed as "to enter into the symbiosis, be there, and emerge from it again". The completion of the symbiosis is necessary for basic security, which again makes it possible to break it. Separation afterwards is necessary in order (in time) to become oneself.

2. *The anal phase, at the age of two to four years*: the task of development during this stage is to learn the art of mastery. To an increasing extent, the child will meet the surrounding world with its demand for control. Control of faeces and strong feelings and impulses are a fundamental demand in a social connection. This is the start of the development of the ego.

3. *The phallic phase, aged four to five*: in this period the child must learn the difference between genders, and the love relationship with its parents must be differentiated. Girls must transfer the object of their love from mother to father, and boys will discover that their fathers are rivals—they fight for the mother. Thus, the question of mastery—phallic sexuality—is still a theme, and the task of development is to survive not having success. In this area, mastery must be submitted to the parents.

4. *The genital phase, puberty*: the task is to conclude the phallic sexuality, which is to be replaced by genital sexuality: that is, directed towards the sex organs and a motile arousal of orgasm. The other, earlier gratifications of drives—oral and anal—are subordinated to genital gratification.

The personality is, thus, still developing until puberty is over. When, precisely, this is will, of course, vary from individual to individual. Most of those who seek coaching are adults, but there could also be young people who require it: in connection with nervousness about exams, for example. In that case, it should be considered whether psychodynamic coaching is the answer, and bear in mind that young people are not fully developed (even if they think so themselves) and, therefore, the work must be carried out differently. Freud believes that each of the phases of development has contributed a layer in the structure of personality, and once it is laid down in the psyche, it does not disappear. If something is inaccessible to consciousness, it is because the later deposits have covered earlier ones. There are older and newer layers, and connections can be made between them, through which modifications are possible (Olsen, 2002). By working with these structures, uncovering the unconscious layers, modifications such as development and change are possible. When the personality is fully developed, it consists of three components: the id, the ego, and the superego. The id is the psychological energy or drive; the ego is the element that relates to the surroundings (the environment), and the superego represents moral precepts, our conscience and ideal aspirations. In other words, it is the ideal ego or ideal self, and the image of ourselves we try to live up to. The task of the ego is to solve the conflicts between drives (the id) and precepts and ideals (the superego). Solving this conflict is the precondition for being able to act. It ensures that, on the one hand, we do not step too far out of line socially to gratify our needs (e.g., by stealing or resorting to violence), and, on the other hand, we do not become passive and dependent, waiting for others to obtain things for us that we cannot manage to obtain for ourselves in the proper manner. The ego relates itself to reality and tries to create gratification within socially acceptable limits. It can be a demanding task for the ego to "negotiate" between the id and the superego. If it becomes too much of a strain, the ego makes use of defence mechanisms. To put it in a popular way, one could say that we develop defence mechanisms in order to withstand the inevitable discomfort of being human. It is necessary to have defence mechanisms. A defence is set up because it must protect and defend us against something. That "something" is fear of whatever it might be. It could be fear of something specific in our surroundings, and in the way the surroundings react. It could also be fear of condemnation from an impulse of conscience from the superego. Finally, it could be the fear of an impulse from the id that cannot be controlled. A misunderstanding that often arises from lack of knowledge in connection with the process of personal development is the belief that defence mechanisms *solely* block development, and it is important to break them down. This is unwise, and, fortunately, not possible. Personal development involves working with the defences. Our defences are part of our personality, and are part of the way we relate to the world. Acknowledging that we are dealing with a defence mechanism and working away from it is quite demanding and associated with many feelings and considerable psychological effort. There is, after all, a reason why we defend ourselves in a particular way, and that is why it is difficult to give it up. When the ego is put under too much strain and the defence mechanism is inadequate, this is referred to in psychodynamic terminology as a lack of ego strength, or as ego weakness. Ego strength denotes the ability to act in relation to a specific reality. In connection with psychodynamic coaching, the reason for coming to the coach might be precisely that the person's defence mechanisms are no longer adequate, and therefore it is difficult to act.

Example

Hans was the leading consultant in an anaesthesiology department, and for a couple of years had understood and explained a conflict with the surgical department as a situation where "they" (the surgical department), personified as certain particular people, had been unwilling to pursue the objectives of the operating theatre, preferring to enjoy their own personal privileges and freedom to come and go as they pleased. They had been inflexible in the general working relationship. The problem in question was that that they cancelled operations, thus obstructing the anaesthetists' planning. Special theme days and development days had been held with teamwork in focus, and there had been a number of meetings between Hans and the management of the surgical department. On these occasions, it had become clear to Hans that there had also been dishonesty and irresponsibility among the anaesthetists. The detailed data about operations cancelled because of anaesthetists shocked him. In connection with his coaching process, he had to take at least two defence mechanisms into consideration: *denial*—his own denial of faults in his own group, and *projec-*

tion—attempting to get rid of the presence of dishonesty and irresponsibility by transference to the surgeons. This discovery swept Hans off his feet. To begin with, he was surprised and angry. He tried to find someone who had concealed the data from him. When he saw it was impossible (he had, in fact, had the data, and kept them at a distance himself), his state of mind changed to embarrassment and shame. He felt he had been caught out, also in relation to himself. His only thought had been that in that case he must pack up and resign. His superego had condemned him. A third defence mechanism also came into play, associated with the other two: *splitting*. He was splitting things into good and bad. Either the surgeons were "bad" (dishonest and irresponsible) or else the anaesthetists must be. The idea that there could be both responsibility and irresponsibility and elements of dishonesty in both departments at the same time was too complicated. How, then, could he lead his department? Being able to understand his defence mechanisms and the way they were fed by group dynamics between the two departments became the subject Hans had to work on, before a new idea could arise about how he then could lead the department.

Thus, defence mechanisms comprise the duality that they make action possible in situations that would otherwise be full of anxiety, but they are also a hindrance because they do not relate to the underlying cause of the anxiety, and the fact that forms of action can be developed that work in the face of reality. Defence mechanisms are an unconscious psychological reaction, so the individual does not know that they are active.

The defence mechanisms in everyday life manifest themselves in different ways (Olsen, 2002):

- *suppression*, as when a client spontaneously says, for instance, "This is not about anger." Then anger is precisely what it is about: the defence is in the "not";
- *devaluation/idealization*, two phenomena that are linked. As a rule with another person, he/she is idealized to begin with and almost becomes a god, and then, when that person proves not to be a god, but simply human, he or she is devalued, and, in other words, is now regarded as having no value at all;
- *denial*, refusing to admit the existence of a real object or phenomenon;

- *repression*, which must prevent gratification of drives by referring concepts or wishes associated with conflict to the unconscious to prevent, for instance, sexual desires from coming to the surface;
- *intellectualizing*, where emotions are excluded from a given situation and it is only treated intellectually;
- *isolation*, which replaces repression by separating feelings and thoughts from each other in such a way that the thoughts can be conscious while the associated feelings are unconscious;
- *projection*, where a person rids him/herself of something, like an undesirable quality that can cause anxiety or pain, and transfers—or projects—it to another person.
- *rationalization*, when a person invents some rational reasons for a particular action that in fact came from an unconscious impulse;
- *regression*, when an outer frustration becomes too powerful. It might be an assignment that is too difficult, illness, or a situation full of anxiety. The psyche "regresses", that is, "goes back to a development phase" or re-establishes an earlier, lower organization of the personality structure and functions at that level;
- *splitting*, dissociating emotions or characteristics when keeping them together becomes too great a threat: for example, that one can hate and love the same person.

Other defence mechanisms have also been described, and some of these are more connected with psychopathology than with everyday life. The defence mechanisms mentioned above were not all formulated by Freud. Several theorists have developed the concept and descriptions further. In particular, Anna Freud, Sigmund Freud's daughter, carried out important work on developing the understanding and systematization of defence mechanisms.

The subsequent development work did not involve the understanding of defence mechanisms alone. After Freud, other theorists have added further developments in psychodynamic personality and development theory. These developments create new understandings and possibilities for clinical work, and, thus, also for psychodynamic coaching. The most outstanding personality and development theories will be mentioned briefly below. Others could also have been included, but the ones here have been selected for their relevance to psychodynamic coaching. As for the description of Freud's theory of personality and development, the following short and superficial review can by no means do justice to the individual complexes of theories. It must only be regarded in connection with the purpose of this book: to describe the relevance of linking the target-orientated focus of the method of coaching with the depth of the psychodynamic theories.

Melanie Klein

Klein worked out her development theory over a long period. She returned to it and developed it further on several occasions, and what she began in 1919 was finally reorganized in 1952. Klein was concerned with the very earliest period in life: the inner world of the infant and its interplay with the external world. Klein's theory is called the object relations theory precisely because it deals with the infant's orientation to the external object. The external object might be part of another person, or the whole person. Klein's theory is built on Freud and on treatment, among other things, through play therapy and analysis of young infants, up to the age of two years. As the years passed, she diverged increasingly from Freud and developed concepts that were entirely her own. Klein was a contemporary of Anna Freud, and they competed as to which of them was most Freudian. This difference of opinion can still be traced in circles working with psychoanalysis right up to the present.

Many different factors associated with Klein and her life and work give insights into the psychoanalytical environment and its history. But, in accordance with the purpose of this book, I focus below on the theories of personality and development, as they are relevant to the practice of psychodynamic coaching. Fantasies are a central concept for Klein. She took these over from Freud, but she attaches more importance to the concept, which is expanded to include unconscious fantasies. Unconscious fantasies are psychological expressions of instincts, and they are always active in everyone right from birth (Hinshelwood 1991; Klein, 1990; Mortensen, 2001). The newborn child is assumed to have a rudimentary ego from the beginning, and this is the basis for the presence of fantasies. The first fantasies are characterized by inability to distinguish between reality and fantasy. They are omnipotent and oral, which means they focus on incorporation and expulsion of objects. This is the preliminary stage of projection and introjection. Fantasies are not necessarily unhealthy, nor are they a defence mechanism. They might be, but they are primarily attendant phenomena (Mortensen, 2001) with all activity in children and adults. Permanent fantasies about the ego and inner objects determine the structure of the personality.

To begin with, Klein thought that development takes place in phases, but, through her observations, she could see that the phases overlap, and this forms the basis for the concept of positions. Positions are both specific characteristic mental stages in the development of the infant, and also general ways of functioning mentally throughout adult life. Thus, Klein sees that there is a direct connection from the course of the original state from childhood to the adult, who, for example, may be "caught" in the paranoid–schizoid position. This is where it becomes relevant in connection with psychodynamic coaching. Klein operates with two positions: the paranoid–schizoid and the depressive. The paranoid–schizoid is the only position in the first period, and it is seen in the infant aged between three and five months, when the baby orientates itself towards part of the mother, the breast, being unable to perceive the whole of the mother all at once. When the breast is present, it is a good object, because it gratifies the child's needs. When it is absent, it is a bad object, and is perceived as persecuting and destructive. The experience is a merging of fantasy and reality. In order to cope with this threatening experience (persecution anxiety), the infant develops a schizoid defence mechanism: splitting. Splitting is the separation of good and evil. Thus, the good object is experienced as separated from the bad object. However, through cognitive development, the child is gradually enabled to perceive the mother as a whole object, which forces the infant to face the reality that good and bad are connected. This brings the infant into the depressive position that is seen at about ten months. In the infant's fantasy, hate for the bad object can now threaten the good object. As a defence against this fear of destruction, the wish to repair arises, which develops consideration and care for the object. Separation anxiety arises in this period, when the child is afraid that the mother has gone forever because the child has destroyed her. Both positions are necessary for development. The depressive position makes it possible to integrate the different components within the child through reparation, when the child gains confidence that its love is stronger than hate.

Development—also later in life—can be understood as alternating between these two positions. In psychodynamic coaching, the development process that takes place can be understood as the process that moves an individual from a paranoid–schizoid position to a depressive position. That is what happens when a perspective opens up and it is possible for the client to move away from the black or white experience of factors to a more differentiated experience, where there is room for many nuances, both in relation to the outside and inside the client. It often feels paralysing at first, but, as they are worked through, several differentiated possibilities for action will appear, some more suitable than others. This process also leads to a change in the client's opinion of him/herself, which can be considered a kind of "proof" of the connection between the perception of inner objects and the external world. The relationship between fantasy and reality is quite crucial in psychodynamic coaching, where the client's ability to observe and register fantasies precisely as fantasies is strengthened. It often leads to a desire to test these fantasies in reality, and, thus, gather new experiences.

Projective identification is another central concept that originates from Klein's development theory. Klein sees projection both as a means of communication between the child and its mother and as a defence mechanism. The first part of the course of events is a projection, when, for instance, the child wants to relieve itself of the feeling of anxiety and thus sends what is threatening (an evil inner object) unconsciously to the mother. As the recipient of the projection, the mother can react in two ways: (1) take it in, process it, and react appropriately—comfort and soothe the child, or (2) if she cannot accommodate it, she can withdraw and thus leave the child with the feeling of anxiety. The child introjects the feeling, that is, draws it into itself, but now in an intensified form. The course taken by this unconscious communication between mother and child will leave its mark on the child later on. Projective identification is a psychological phenomenon that requires two people. Every one of us bears the traces of the original unconscious projective communication that went on between our mothers and ourselves. Chapter Four gives a more detailed description of how projective identification arises and plays a part in the everyday lives of adults who have to work together.

Klein's theories and concepts contribute to the probability that the patterns we play over in relation to authorities over us are linked to the course taken by the interaction with the original authorities.

Margaret Mahler

In her work, Mahler concentrated on the first three years of a child's life. Mahler's starting point is Freud's theory of drives about personality and development, but she divides the period up into a larger number of shorter phases than Freud. Mahler's theory is a theory of phases, which means she divides the first three years into different periods that are limited in time, and each has its psychological development task. In general, one could say that what Mahler is concerned with is how the child becomes itself, or how it individualizes. Her theory is based on empirical studies of the relation between mother and child, since this is the relationship in which development tasks are linked together. Mahler's extensive and thorough empirical studies were particularly epoch making, and she laid the foundations for a great deal of later research through this "baby watching" method. She speaks of the child's two births, the physical and the psychological birth. The psychological birth is the one that lasts through the first three years of life, and the psychological processes are closely associated with the physical birth. The first phase is the autistic phase, in the first month of life. The autistic state should not be understood in the way it is used diagnostically, but rather as a state of self-sufficiency, where the child is occupied with its inner self and not with the outer world.

The next phase is the symbiotic state, which lasts from the age of two months to five months. The child is now occupied with something from the outer world: this is the breast and, thus, the mother as part object. The child feels it is a single unit with the mother. The child cannot differentiate what is its mother and what is the child itself. It is important that this phase allows for symbiosis, or that the mother satisfies the child's needs for closeness, for instance through breast-feeding, so that this phase is characterized by the satisfaction and omnipotence on which the basal experience of security is founded. However, a good symbiosis does not arise purely from physical proximity. There must be psychological presence, calm and concentration at the same time. This phase forms the crucial background for the next phase, which lasts from the age of five to ten months. In this third phase, the theme is differentiation. The child must be "hatched" (Mahler, Pine, & Bergman, 1975), or separated from the mother, and learn to distinguish between the mother and itself. The mother's task in the relationship is to make this possible for the child. Through this phase, the mother becomes a complete object and is not, as before, a part-object.

The next phase, the fourth, lasts from ten to eighteen months, and is called the practising phase, when one could say that it must ratify that the child is an independent person who can venture out into the world and explore it. This phase coincides with the physical stage when the child begins to walk, at the same time as the psychological "going out into the world". The world is exciting, and almost makes the child feel ecstatic and full of omnipotent sensations and feelings. This also coincides with what Freud called the narcissistic phase. Momentarily, when the mother is out of reach, the child will make contact with the fact that something is missing, which it formerly considered as the other half of itself (the mother as part-object), and this results in mood changes from exultation to subdued. The subdued moods result from the child's attempts to handle the pain by turning its attention inwards and forming an inner picture or representation of its mother. Transitional objects, such as soft toys, blankets, a dummy, or the like might be useful to help the child to deal with the deprivation and soothe itself. The child's capacity for this depends on the earlier phases.

The fifth and last-but-one phase is the rapprochement phase, which lasts until the age of twenty-four months. In this phase, the child is confronted with the reality that "The world is very big and I am very little." This assimilation of the reality becomes an emotional turning point, which is important for the later self-image. The child experiences and understands that the mother is not always nearby, and it causes pain and privation. The child also acknowledges that it wants to explore the world and try out its capabilities. The child experiences emotional ambivalence, wanting both to be one with its mother and to be separate from her. The child tries to deal with this in different ways. The more the mother is emotionally available, the better chances the child has of finding "solutions" to this ambivalence. In this phase, the child develops many of the new functions of the ego and needs to have psychological energy available for this. If the rapprochement phase proved to be characterized by crisis during this development, there will be too little energy for developing the ego, which could later have consequences for the strength of the ego.

The final phase is the consolidation phase, which runs from the second year into the third year. In this period, the development task for the child is to attain a more solid individuality and achieve object constancy. Object constancy is the inner, internalized "picture" of the mother, which soothes anxiety and pain and makes it possible to act in tense states or situations. Mahler concluded that, after the third year, children—precisely because they have achieved individuality—develop differently, and, therefore, it is not possible to describe anything general. Children extend the meaningful relations to more people beside the mother, and orientate themselves more and more to the social systems that make up the surrounding environment.

It will be obvious that Mahler's observations and theories are useful in clinical connections, and the way she developed the theory further has contributed to qualifying the overall psychodynamic development theory. Later, there were other empirically based theoretical developments which changed some of Mahler's ideas with regard to the first phases, but these will be commented on in the following sections.

So, what significance can Mahler have for psychodynamic coaching? In addition to increasing the underlying understanding of both the history of psychodynamic theory and of the formation and development of each individual, Mahler is interesting because of her understanding of just how deeply seated our relationship to closeness and separation is, and, thus, how important an element it is in our development of autonomy.

In a postmodern (working) life we enter into relationships all the time. At the tangible level, we communicate with many people all the time. Our work consists of a spider's web of dependencies on what others do or do not do. Not just locally, but globally, too. Psychologically, we need other people and close relationships. In postmodern life there is a predominant, culturally determined focus on the autonomous individual's distinctive characteristics (Jørgensen, 2002). Jørgensen formulates the question of development that appears more than any other on the postmodern agenda: "How can independence, self-reliance and autonomy be developed, and how can the possibility of self-realization be opened up, while at the same time the individual remains emotionally linked to others?" (Jørgensen, 2002, p. 216) This problem occurs, for instance, in different forms in connection with management. Most managers have found that they can only succeed if they can persuade others—their employees—to do something specific that harmonizes with the overall objective of the main assignment. Following a manager's leadership, or the willingness to provide company, depends on the relationship between the manager and employee. This relationship is determined by the material exchange relation and the relation of power and authority, but probably also to an equal extent by the emotional relationship, which partly determines the degree of security, confidence, openness, and equality. It is vital for a manager that he or she can create and maintain emotional connections.

This also applies to relationships of working together, and one could say that it is one of the acknowledged facts of life that almost anything can be achieved if we do it willingly together, and that almost nothing can be done if we are unwilling. The emotionally healthy relation is precisely one that balances between autonomy and independence. Holding on to one's individuality and realizing one's potential while at the same time holding on to considerate and meaningful relationships is attractive both at work and in private life. The seeds are sown during the first three years of life, and Mahler's contribution is a way of understanding how far this seed has been nurtured and ripened in a healthy direction or not.

Example

Simon was the deputy headmaster of a school. He and the headmaster were jointly the senior leaders of the school. Simon was the administrative leader and the head was in charge of the educational side. Simon asked for coaching because he had repeatedly been in conflict with the teachers about their working hours and terms of employment. The headmaster recommended that Simon should seek help, because he valued Simon's professional approach highly. In several ways Simon had "saved" the school, which had suffered from a chaotic administrative situation under the previous deputy headmaster, who was, in fact, dismissed because of abuse. Besides, the headmaster was a declared believer in solving conflicts. "Nothing is insoluble if you speak from the heart and listen with your heart," as he said. Simon was irritated by the teachers, who did not observe the administrative rules, did not register things as they should, and were lax and sloppy. They would forget the receipts when they claimed for expenses, or did not notify him in time about what courses they planned to attend and when they would be away.

"How are they ever going to get a sense of order into the children's heads, when they are so irresponsible themselves, because there must be a connection, surely?" he asked. The conflicts arose most frequently at meetings of the Education Committee. There had been many episodes in connection with the teachers' laxity and neglect that had ended with sparks flying. Simon would become very angry, shout, and accuse the teachers of not living up to their positions and being unco-operative, and he would finally leave the meeting with remarks like: "If you can't stand the heat, you should get out of the kitchen!" Simon always regretted these outbursts afterwards, but could not control his temperament. His goal for psychodynamic coaching was to gain better control, so that he could keep command in these situations and find an inner calm to work out some better checking systems to ensure that the administrative routines actually became routines for everyone.

Simon's CV was characterized by a number of appointments inter-spersed with longish breaks, when he had taken supplementary train-ing or travelled. He was aware of the problem about his temperament from previous situations. Simon's style of management was authori-tarian, and he had difficulty with ambiguities. Direct orders or penal-ties were the solutions he could understand in connection with the teachers' negligence. He had cancelled grants for courses, for instance, to penalize teachers who did not notify him before the deadline of when they wanted to take holidays. He could not accommodate the idea that it is possible to be sloppy in some areas and conscientious in others. He divided the group of teachers into those he liked and those he disliked. Anyone who let down the side was "sent out" and could not get back into his good books again. Simon had originally been a teacher, but did not get on with the children and their parents, where the same pattern had shown up. His private life was also character-ized by an "either/or" approach. He set high standards for himself with regard to being a good friend and a responsible partner who did not let anyone down. He kept agreements and was faithful and punc-tual. However, he had replaced everything in his life—resigned from his job, left his partner, and moved away from his circle of friends—as many as three times. He had no children, because he did not believe that he could find a woman in whom he had enough faith for that "project" to have any chance of success.

Seen through Mahler's eyes, Simon was struggling with the con-sequences of not having confidence in the world and in other people, a fragile inner object, and an imbalance between separation and involvement. The consequences were low tolerance of ambiguity, a penalizing superego, and psychological inflexibility. The way for Simon to develop lay in the fact that he also had longings. He longed for closeness, and carried within him a grief for the good object he had lost, which, therefore, was not internalized either. It turned out that Simon had had a very young mother, who, for long periods, had been unable to look after him properly and care for him. The symbiosis had never been established, and this had affected the following phases. Simon's defence was revenge or withdrawal. His father had been stable and present, but also affected by the unsatisfactory marriage, which left him weak and indulgent. Simon needed to go through a process of grieving in order to develop. He had to make contact with his grief and an anger that he had always tried—with success—to repress. Through coaching, however, it became clear to him that there was an emotionally logical connection between his childhood, his management style, his lifestyle, and his longing for closeness.

D. W. Winnicott

Winnicott was a paediatrician and psychoanalyst who was inspired by Klein. He did not develop an independent theory of development or personality, but contributed some important concepts that are extremely valuable when applied in connection with psychodynamic coaching. He worked on the development of the self—the ego in action. How is the ego enabled to settle the conflict between the super-ego and the id, so that it is able to act? What is involved in psycho-dynamic coaching is often a question of how clients, through cognitive and emotional insights and understanding, can be enabled to act differently in their lives from the way in which their repetitive urge determines. Winnicott formulated the concepts of the true and false self. The false self appears when the child needs to adapt itself too early to other people's demands and pressures. The child will then become estranged from its own experiences and feelings. The true self develops when the child's parents succeed in creating a "transitional area" for the child. This transitional area is the phase when the child must make the transition from an omnipotent perception of itself to a reality-based perception. Through the omnipotent perception, the child sees itself as all-powerful, as if it had itself created everything good, including its mother's breast that provides milk. The transitional area is the field of dynamic tension between fantasy and reality. Play is often the method by which the child comes to terms with its experiences and impressions. Transitional objects are things that help the child through this phase. A transitional object might be a blanket, something to suck or bite on, a rag doll, or a cuddly toy. The transitional object forms a bridge between the inner and outer reality. This transitional bridge can comfort the child, or the child can confide feelings to the transitional object, and transitional objects might often be subjected to violent attacks from the child, thus providing a means of dealing with aggression. The surrounding environment created by the parents in this phase is highly significant. Winnicott formed the concept of the "good-enough mother", which means the caring, attentive, and accommodating mother, who first can create the omnipotent phase where the child feels all-powerful, and then initiate an adapted and targeted process in which the child is confronted with reality. Winnicott called the overall concept of the good environment for children a "holding environment". Parents can help the child in the transitional area first and foremost by being aware of how sensitive this period is for the child, and how important the transitional object is. The child can be stimulated in its working process through participation in play.

In connection with psychodynamic coaching, one meets clients who, in fact, cannot sense how they feel, or who are extremely uncertain about their own experiences. There might be mild manifestations of a false self. This can be investigated in connection with the personal history and the interpretation can be shared with the clients, who must then work on it and practise feeling their impulses and discussing experiences, and must be supported in finding themselves, or their selves.

Erik Erikson

Erikson was occupied with the part of the personality which Freud called the ego, and of the work of the ego to define and maintain its identity (Brørup, Hauge, & Lyager Thomsen, 1993; Carver & Scheier, 1992; Erikson, 1977; Mortensen, 2001). Erikson developed the idea of development phases further to an epigenetic model. At the beginning, the phases follow the psychosexual development, but Erikson thinks of development further through life than to the end of puberty. This is connected with Erikson's ideas of personality development—understood as the formation of the ego—as the result of three organizational processes: a biological process to ensure the development of the body; a psychological process to ensure the organization of the individual ego; a social process that develops a cultural relationship of belonging to groups. These three processes are mutually connected, so that changes in one of these processes will lead to changes in the other processes. Erikson developed theories about several psychological factors, but is best known for his phase model. He divided development into eight phases. Each phase is characterized by a development task that the individual must carry out. The way in which each individual meets this challenge of development becomes a determining platform for the way the next developmental task is achieved. The first developmental task (from birth to one year old) is concerned with the degree to which fundamental confidence is established. It is primarily a question of the quality of the relationship between mother and child. The child is at the mercy of the mother or the person who is in the mother's place.

The next stage (age one to three years) is about daring to go out into the world by letting go of the mother. Here, it can be seen very clearly how the achievement of one step determines the success of the next. Whether the child dares to let go of the mother depends on what confidence the child has in the world. Can the world be relied on as a good enough place, and is the child good enough to make his/her own decisions? The development task of this second step is concerned with independence and self-control. Can one go out into the world alone and do anything without losing one's self-esteem? If the feeling of self-esteem is lost, the result is a feeling of shame and self-doubt.

The challenge at the third step (age three to five years) is to conquer the world predominantly successfully. The child must learn to take initiatives and observe limits, not only those set by its mother and father, but those of other authorities, such as other family members, kindergarten staff, and leaders of leisure activities. Taking initiatives that one can cope with and carry out without setbacks or feelings of guilt if they do not succeed entirely. This age coincides with the Oedipal phase, precisely where defeat must be accepted, with the knowledge that the child's father or mother cannot be put out of the running. But this necessary defeat must fall into place in a way that does not damage the self-image. This is the phase when the child develops its superego, that is, learns to sense what is right and good, or bad and wrong. Many parents will be able to recognize the experience of the child as "policeman" in dealings with adults, other children, and itself.

The fourth phase stretches over a long time, from the age of six to the beginning of puberty. This is when everything that has been developed and experienced so far is consolidated. More and more demands will be made of the child, both at school and in the other systems of which the child is a part. The development task is to find a balance in relation to capability. The optimal situation is to gain experiences of being able to work and unfold in ways that develop a sense of self-esteem and competence. There is a risk, however, that the result will be feelings of inferiority and negative expectations of oneself instead. Unlike Freud, Erikson considered that there was a good deal of activity in this period, and Erikson did not see it primarily as building up to the next period: puberty.

In this fifth phase, the necessary changes place considerable demands on the child, who must now become adult. The psychological changes occur at the same time as physiological and hormonal changes in the body. This is the phase where the heading is identity, where the young person is working on "Who am I?" Gender identity and sexuality are themes in the spotlight. The group of friends plays a crucial role. Young people's experiments with "What type of person am I?" manifest themselves as rapid changes of clothing, music, and language. The themes of the other phases are reactivated, and many of the fundamental questions are raised again by the young person, internally. The physiological system settles down and the personality is in a more settled framework, but there are still developmental psychological projects in adult life, too.

Erikson divided adult life into three phases, without indication of age: the *early adult years*, when the task is to be able to enter into love relationships without melting entirely together with the other person, or withdrawing—to be able to isolate one's feelings; the *adult years*, when the task is concerned with expanding the ego's interests to set up a family and have children. The psychological part of it is to be caring, be responsible for and provide for others, and enjoy it as an enrichment of life. This is the opposite of coming to a halt. In the third adult stage, *old age*, the task is to achieve integrity, and to see and understand oneself and one's life in a larger, meaningful perspective, without giving up in despair or becoming bitter.

Erikson's model is helpful in several ways in connection with psychodynamic coaching. The great majority of those who seek coaching are adults who have jobs and children, and who, thereby, have obligations of an emotional and material nature. In connection with changes that are imposed from outside, a common occurrence in postmodern working life, human identity comes up on the agenda. We often identify ourselves with our professionalism, our job and workplace, and the work we do. Changes in these also affect our identity: if I am not employed here, who am I, in fact? If I am not the person who carries out these assignments, who am I, in fact? And so on. In connection with technological developments and globalization, very large numbers of people find their tasks and their work being changed fundamentally. We find psychological balances in relation to the person we have, in fact, become, but when involuntary changes are made in our lives, all our development themes are reactivated. In this connection, Erikson's model gives an interesting picture of what we have to cope with psychologically, while, at the same time, we are adults, go to work, and function as breadwinners, and so on. It might seem like a developmental crisis, and, thus, it will also present the possibilities of a crisis through reactivating the fundamental identity themes of earlier phases for finding a new, more mature, and satisfactory level of identity.

Example

Hannah was a chemical engineer, and, until the end of the previous year, had been the manager of the development section in a major pharmaceutical company with a global market. At the end of the year, the senior management implemented a structural reorganization in the company, an adaptation to demanding global competition. The company needed to be geared to faster product development, with more rapid processes from development to production, and with high, easily adjustable quality control. This was done by introducing a flat matrix organization, which supported easier and more direct communications between various employees with different professional specialities by limiting the number of managers and upgrading the project method of operation. In this connection, Hannah's position was phased out, and the work of the development section was taken over by project managers who led and co-ordinated it. Hannah's new job was a specialist function, and in this capacity she was involved with various projects. In her private life, Hannah had a successful marriage, and her twin sons had finished at sixth-form college the previous year. One was travelling abroad and the other had moved into town to study. Hannah came for coaching because she was not satisfied with her work situation. She had lost her inspiration, and wanted help to find the direction she should take work-wise. She was forty-six, and had made an excellent career that was far from culminating. She had held a research post at the university for several years, and then, five years ago, she took up a leading position in a private company. She had achieved solid results in both positions.

Through psychodynamic coaching, it became obvious that Hannah was struggling with a complex of identity problems. During the past year, she had lost two essential roles in her life: the role of a mother with children living at home, and her management job. Neither of these changes happened at her initiative, but were the consequences of developments that could not be avoided, even if they were fore-seeable. Both came as a shock to Hannah, however. Or, rather, what came as a shock to her was what they *meant*. She had felt it as a defeat, and it gave her inferior thoughts about her own worth: suddenly, she felt as if she were nothing, or worthless and full of the idea that it was impossible for her to be "chosen" as a desirable person. "It's every man for himself, and you just have to look after your own affairs and interests," as she put it, bitterly. In other words, Hannah had come up against development themes from earlier phases in life as a develop-ment task, and it was a task she did not want. What she had to work through once again was: can one have confidence in anything at all? Can I achieve anything worthwhile, or was it all bluff? How humili-ating it is to be dismissed from a manager position—what am I to tell other people? It had become too difficult, and she had, therefore, become more and more introverted, losing interest in seeing friends as before. Hannah wanted to get back to her earlier state, but that was impossible. She simply had to confront herself in a new and more conscious manner with her self and who she really was.

John Bowlby

Bowlby's theory of attachment and inner working models is interesting in several ways in connection with psychodynamic coaching, because the understanding of an individual's self-image and self-esteem is given depth, as it is linked to the personal history. The theory is also interesting because, on the one hand, Bowlby is aware that the inner structures are relatively permanent, but that, on the other hand, it is possible to change and develop them in a healthier and more satisfactory direction. Bowlby was originally inspired by Klein's theories, but became more and more interested in the significance of the actual family situation in the development of the individual. In the theory of drives, the child's dependency on, and attachment to, the mother is primarily attributed to the mother's function in gratifying urges through breast-feeding. In object relation theory, attachment is also understood as a result of a driving need for relationships. Bowlby abandons Freud's starting point in physical causes (regarding psychological energy and drives) in favour of the tradition of behaviour study in biology (Mortensen, 2001). Bowlby shows, through the experiments of others, that attachment and food are not linked. He leaves the phase theory and focuses instead on the theory of paths of development, which considers human personality as a structure undergoing constant development. To begin with, there are many mutually separated paths to choose between, but as time passes, the paths are differentiated more and more, and the number of open paths is reduced (Mortensen, 2001; Waddington, 1957). This is the biological starting point; in other words, what is inherited determines the number of possibilities at the beginning of life. It is the environment that determines the choice of paths. The environment is understood as the quality of relationships and, thus, the possibility for development and attachment.

The capacity for forming attachments is considered a sign of psychological health. Bowlby called the successful process and establishment of the ability to form attachments "secure attachment". He distinguished between the concepts of attachment and attachment behaviour. In humans, attachment is an innate and fundamental need. Humans form bonds with other selected individuals, and show attachment behaviour even as infants. Attachment behaviour can, for instance, take the form of crying, calling, smiling, whimpering (signal behaviour), or attempts to follow and cling (rapprochement behaviour) (Beck, 2006). This is to ensure that a security-regulating system of behaviour is developed, supposedly to protect the child. The attachment system allows the child to regulate the availability of the attachment figure, normally the mother. The attachment figure is the secure base from which the child can explore the world. If there is any "danger", the attachment system is activated and attachment behaviour takes over. The patterns of interaction that arise between the child and the attachment figure are internalized and form the basis of experience for expectations of other coming relationships. This internalization develops into mental representations, which Bowlby called inner working models. Internalization becomes part of the personality, as the way the person relates to others.

In connection with psychodynamic coaching, it is interesting that these working models *can* be changed later in life in connection with new experiences. It is not something that happens easily; the working models are unconscious, automatic, and fairly robust (Beck, 2006; Mortensen, 2001). It can be done, but the changes have to be made in another relationship that is qualitatively different from the original, a relationship where new awareness can arise and new experiences can be made. The working models are organized at different levels in the personality, which contains both general and more specific assumptions. To what extent an individual feels lovable and certain that there will be someone to help if he/she needs it is, thus, "printed" in the inner working model. As understood by Bowlby, the purpose of the defence mechanisms is to ensure that information that could disturb the working model does not reach consciousness. This, then, is the resistance that the coach will meet in the client. Bowlby identifies two ways in which the defence can appear: (1) evasively, where the child suppresses its own needs because unconsciously it imagines that a refusal will follow; (2) ambivalence, where the child clings to the adult because it is afraid of being left alone.

Mary Ainsworth, who carried the work on the attachment theory further, has produced valuable empirical research in connection with defining different attachment patterns, and, in extension of this, developed a so-called "strange situation test" that can provide data about a child's attachment pattern. Using this, four different types of attachment patterns could be identified: (1) the fearful–rejecting type; (2) the secure type; (3) the fearful–ambivalent type; (4) the fearful–disorganized type.

There is, of course, a great difference between the use of these tests in a clinical situation with patients who are to be diagnosed and treated and using the tests in connection with personal development in normally functioning individuals. Nevertheless, the concepts are useful in connection with finding where the focus should be in a course of coaching. When there is a wish for progress career-wise, it is necessary to have the courage to take the necessary actions, such as writing applications, making contacts, cultivating networks, and taking initiatives that can bring oneself into the desired situation. In this connection, the client's relational competencies, including self-confidence and expectations of the results, are highly significant.

If a person expects a rejection and would really prefer to avoid the risk, then there is less likelihood of moving up in the hierarchy than if a good result is expected and the person is relaxed and open in a contact situation. A given attachment pattern and working model, with the associated self-image and self-confidence, can, therefore, be self-reinforcing. Attachment situations must be "re-experienced" emotionally and cognitively reworked before they can be broken. Here, the relationship with the coach is a possibility. Through his/her data, including observations from countertransference, the coach can get a better idea of which working model the client has and share information with the client, who will then have a chance, together with the coach, to investigate the historical connections and the way they manifest themselves in the present. Insights into attachment patterns are also interesting for managers in relation to their employees. With this insight, problems with employees can, on some occasions, appear in a completely different light. Withdrawal, shyness, and low self-esteem can look like intolerance and superciliousness, and the actions a manager will take will be very different in the two situations. Some managers struggle with particular types of employees, and here, too, insight and increased emotional awareness can be a help.

Example

Susan was the office manager in a manufacturing company where there were many women employed part-time and paid by the hour. Having so many part-time employees gave rise to many problems, because there were three-shift operations at the same time. When Susan had to explain the problem, she said that it was quite simply a situation where she ended up saying yes when she ought to say no to new requests for reduction of hours. It was one type of employee in particular that she had difficulty in tackling, in maintaining her demands for full-time work. "It is those weepy types," she said, in quite a hard tone. "I simply cannot take it, so I agree to what they want, just to get them out of my way as fast as possible." Susan never allows herself to go round and whine, as she put it. It turned out that the aversion to whining and weepy types was both a real and a reality-orientated problem. If employees are unhappy and dissatisfied with their work, it is not good for them, or for the atmosphere of the workplace. It was also a projective phenomenon for Susan. She hated and denied the existence of her own weaker sides. She had always pulled herself together and managed whatever needed to be done, and did not go round asking for help all the time. During the course of coaching, Susan also realized how much loneliness this entailed, and that it was linked to the whole of her childhood and a frustrating relationship with demanding and inattentive parents, who had hoped for a boy instead of her. Part of Susan's self-esteem was a sort of "self-esteem in defiance", concealing at its centre a very small Susan who longed for real recognition, closeness, and acceptance, even when she was not the big girl who coped with everything. Her method of getting her need for relationships covered consisted of "not being a nuisance" behaviour, and "I can manage everything without problems and whining" behaviour. It was an adaptation to the surrounding environment, which had led to attachment disturbances that were not pathological, but still serious, and a subsequent slight false self, in Winnicott's sense.

As a result of the course of coaching, Susan wanted to continue working with this situation in therapy, because she discovered how many areas there were where it was an obstacle to the things she really wanted out of life, such as her relationships with men and having her own family. Her expectations that it could succeed for her and that she could be a good mother were very slight, and this had prevented her from ever considering it seriously. But she still longed for it.

Heinz Kohut

Kohut's psychology of the self extends the psychodynamic understanding of personality once again. His theory developed against the background of analysing adult patients with various degrees of narcissistic disturbances. The psychology of the self, which later became an independent discipline, distinguishes itself from the theories outlined so far: the theory of drives, the object relation theory, and the psychology of the ego. Up to now, the self has been understood as the ego in action. Kohut defines the self as an overall designation for the whole of the psychological structure, the personality, and they are both formed through early relationships. Children are born with narcissistic needs that must be satisfied by others. These are not just any others, but specific others, normally the parents. Kohut agrees with the other theoreticians that the newborn infant cannot distinguish between itself and what is its mother. The mother is for the child what Kohut calls a self-object. A self-object is an object that the child imagines to be part of itself, or as an extension of itself (Brørup, Hauge, & Lyager Thomsen, 1993; Carver & Scheier, 1992; Jørgensen, 2002). All humans have self-objects throughout life, and their function is to stabilize the emotional life and psychological makeup.

The self develops through the relationship between the child and significant others. There are two periods: first a grandiose period, when the child perceives itself as the centre of the world and when it idealizes the parent figure, with whom it feels itself interconnected. The illusion arises because the parents reflect the infant as perfect, and admire and encourage it. This satisfies the child's inborn narcissistic needs. The illusion and what is perfect have to be adjusted in the next phase by reality. The child must have its grandiose self-image and the idealizing image of the parents corrected gradually by reality, so that the libido from the grandiose self is added to the real self. By this means, the infant goes through a transforming internalization (Kohut, 1990), which enables it to take care of itself and live with the fact of life that it is not perfect, and neither are its parents perfect. The precondition for healthy development in this phase is empathy and balance in the parents' relationship with the child, so that the child is met with care and attention while being frustrated optimally. The parents must be able to "read" the child's needs and match them in a balanced way—and an infant's needs are different from a schoolchild's needs. It is just as important for the infant's grandiose needs to be satisfied as it is for them to be adjusted later on. If the parents cannot match the child's needs, disturbances can arise that will result in an unrealistic self-image, in a narcissistic disturbance. According to

Kohut, these disturbances can be corrected if the disturbed person is given the opportunity to form new emotional experiences.

Obviously, this line of thought is central for psychodynamic coaching. If the coaching can create new emotional experiences through the client's relationship with the coach or with a third person outside the course of coaching, changes will be possible in the client. The job of a manager is one that often receives a lot of attention, and one might find, therefore, that it almost attracts people who are looking for a narcissistic reflection. If a manager wants this reflection but does not get it, there could be difficulties. They might be personal difficulties for the manager and for employees. In some workplaces, "narcissistic pairs" might also be found, where the manager and the deputy both have a slight narcissistic disturbance, and where they mutually satisfy each other in their reflections. It might work out for a time, and apparently function well, but sooner or later their shortcomings will be exposed and their management will fall apart. The narcissistic disturbance will appear as a disturbed self-image, that is, the individual lives as if he/she was capable of more than in reality. If a child has not been met with empathy in connection with its narcissistic needs and early development, but instead has met with humiliation and lack of empathy and acknowledgement, the defence against the threat might be to turn the situation completely around and live in a constructed reality where inferiority leads to overrating oneself.

What is relevant for psychodynamic coaching in this theory about personality is that if the client has problems with an over-large self-image, it will be relevant to search for data that confirm the difference between the real capacity and competence and the imagined capacity and competence. It can, for instance, be illustrated through the goals the client has had and the results achieved: the more data, the better. Awareness of transference is also important as data. People with a narcissistic disturbance can seem impressive and captivating, but gradually one gets the impression that something is wrong, and disappointment follows, because the narcissist cannot live up to the image presented, the acted figure. Behind the bragging or glittering surface is, in fact, an unhappy person with very low self-esteem and a solid defence against strong feelings like love or grief. In some cases the pain is dulled through abuse, and, as Kohut describes it, the inability to care for oneself is one of the characteristics of the narcissist.

Example

Henry was one of the consultants in a large firm of consultants. He came for his coaching in very casual clothes, almost leisure wear, but they were very expensive. His attitude was friendly, collegial, charming, and slightly over-familiar. He wanted coaching because "there was just something he needed to sort out". Together with two colleagues, he had developed a course of management training for a very large international industrial group. He had had some differences of opinion with the female colleague. They ran a trial course, and after it the clients had reported back that they would like to proceed with the course. However, they had requested that Henry should not be one of the three consultants. Without argument, Henry's director had accepted this and found a different third consultant for the course. It was a large assignment, and it had a considerable effect on Henry's budgeted estimate of earnings in the firm when he lost the assignment, because he then had to spend time on finding another client and developing a new concept for them. His salary was partly on a commission basis, so it also affected his own earnings.

Henry felt aggrieved about the client's assessment of him, and was angry with his director and the colleagues, who had not said a single word to change the decision. He was also annoyed about the financial consequences. The client's evaluation was that Henry did not seem competent enough, and that he was very impetuous in carrying out the sessions of personal supervision that were part of the course. Several of the participants had felt harassed. Henry's explanation was that "direct feedback always results in some resistance", and "after all, people do not always like being told the truth".

He described the progress of his own career. It sounded as if he had done everything really well. He had a commercial education and started as the youngest partner in a firm of consultants, where he learnt to sell and develop concepts and run training courses. He left the firm because he wanted to start his own, and he did so together with a colleague. The colleague did not have much flair for business, so it did not work out very well, and the firm closed down. Henry started again himself—with a big outlay—"because you have to match the clients you want". It was a big office in the inner city, with new design furniture and lamps, and he employed a secretary and four consultants, and so on. "But would you believe it, it got too lonely. I was short of qualified consultants, and did not want to end up in the stress trap. Drowning in your own success—isn't that what it's called? So I sold everything at a good price, and after a sabbatical year, I was employed where I am now."

There was something that did not tally in this story. After considerable further examination of the story, a more truthful picture emerged. He had never completed his education. The partner from the first firm threw him out because he swindled through falsifying documentation. He went bankrupt with the second firm, and was unemployed for a year after that. He was taken on in his present job because a former student friend had put in a good word for him. During his coaching, most of the time was spent on bringing the real story up to the surface and working through the feelings associated with it and the underlying childhood history. It had been a cold and deprived childhood, with plenty of money but no empathy or caring. His mother drank, and his father lived several lives all at once. At the end of this course of coaching, a number of specific tasks were listed, with a view to acquiring some real qualifications, and they formed the basis for a new course of coaching.

Daniel Stern

The work of Stern created completely new insights, knowledge, and practice: a new theory about the very earliest stages of development. Some critics of psychodynamic understanding and practice are known to say that Stern rescued psychoanalysis, implying that otherwise it would have died out because it was old, inapplicable in our time, and uninteresting. It is a point well worth noting that everyone—including theoretical opponents—respects Stern's work. He has indeed had a considerable influence on psychology and educational theory. The other theories that have been mentioned are based on two types of empirical observation: studies of the development of children (the observed child) and deductions about children's development based on analysis, treatment, and the accounts of adults (the clinical child). Stern found that there were many differences between these two types of data, and this became the starting point for his research. He noted and proved that babies experience far more, and in a far more differentiated way, than anyone had previously known. Stern is interesting in connection with psychodynamic coaching, because the formation of the self is described in a far more differentiated way, and it is, therefore, also possible to work with greater precision.

From birth to two months old, the child is in the world of emotions, and from the mother builds up a basic psychological form. This is the foundation for expectations of future relationships. Stern calls what is formed there the emergent self. From two to six months the core self is formed through the child's capacity for social interaction. The child develops an integrated and experiential sense of itself and of others. A healthy core self develops when the mother is able to be present psychologically "here and now" together with the child. Thus, it is not only a question of the mother being with the child, but, to a great extent, of the psychological and emotional quality of the mother's presence. From seven to fifteen months is the period when the child develops the subjective self. The child discovers that it has an inner life that is visible and different from the life inside others. He/she also discovers that what is inside can be shared with others through contact and closeness. This is the background for the later capacity for sharing with others, to share love, fellowship, and closeness with others and, thereby, capacity for empathy.

Language forms the next development, from eighteen to thirty months: the verbal self. The child learns to express itself, and that verbal expression can never completely express the inner meaning; there will always be two versions of the same event: the inner and the expressed version. The verbal tasks the child is given by others help to set the limits for what can be shared and what it is forbidden to share. The family's culture and norms form parallels and ruptures in relation to the child's inner world. From the age of three to four years, children begin to tell stories about themselves and what they have experienced. In this way, the child builds an individual identity. Stern's point is that, on the one hand, he describes in detail how relationships are co-creators of an individual's personality and development, and, on the other hand, how the child's own specific and unique experience of itself is also a co-creator. This can be regarded as attaching greater importance to biology but, at the same time, as a differentiation of the understanding of the importance of the environment. This is why the relational interplay of the sensitivity of the environment, closeness, and empathizing become central factors in a coaching process.

In a process of personal development, the relationship between the client and coach is crucial. If any development is to take place, the coach must be able to establish an environment for healthy development, similar to the one the mother should establish in relation to the child in the original process of formation. The coach's sense and capacity for empathy, mental closeness, and feelings for the client are, therefore, significant. To put it a little bluntly, we could say that it is impossible to develop anyone one does not like. It emphasizes the importance of registering countertransference phenomena, and, in general, of documenting what happens inside the coach in relation to the client. It is not enough to be professional and neutral. One must actually like one's clients. Since the first, trail-blazing works, Stern has written about "the present moment" as a concept that describes what has an effect in a development process between people. It is a valuable concept and description for psychodynamic coaching. This concept illustrates once more the intricacy of the interplay between biology and environment—in this case mirror neurons and psychological closeness.

Theories of personality, development theories, and psychodynamic coaching

As can be seen from the foregoing brief summaries of essential psychodynamic personality and development theories, there are overlaps, while explanations and understandings might conflict, but there is also a common fundamental understanding that originates from Freud: the concept of the unconscious, the importance of emotions and relationships, and the historically defined structure of personality. The common starting point strengthens the way in which the theories supplement each other and deepen the perspective. The strength of psychodynamic coaching is precisely this diversity combined with depth. The detective work the coach and client carry out has many serious sources of inspiration in these theories, and it is important that the coach is familiar with the theories and concepts and how to apply them. The coach's capacity in relation to their application is connected to the coach's background and training. It is necessary, but not in itself sufficient, to have read and understood in order to practise psychodynamic coaching.

The coach's training

Working on other people's wishes for change demands knowledge, insight, courage, and involvement. There is no single specific way of training for working with psychodynamic coaching. A solid theoretical training or supplementary training in psychology, educational theory, or related fields can lay the foundation for further studies and training in the psychological tradition. A course of training over several years, which includes theory, supervision of one's own work, and self-therapy and personal development must be a requirement for the coach. It is not possible to acquire the necessary skills in a short time. Nor can it be done once and for all. Working with other people's development demands constant work with one's own development, both personal and professional. Fortunately, there are a number of suitable possibilities in a number of places round the world where qualifications can be kept up to date and improved. Sharing and reflecting on one's own practice with colleagues should also be a natural part of daily life for a coach practising in psychodynamics. As mentioned before, experience can be a help, but it can also be dangerous, because you think you know. Certainty and authority in the field are necessary, but they must be combined with humility, and this can be acquired through placing oneself regularly in the client's chair.

CHAPTER FOUR

Psychodynamic coaching for couples: the psychology of meeting

W e meet people constantly. We can long for a meeting, feel apprehensive about it, try to avoid a meeting, or try to arrange one. Some meetings are short, while others last a lifetime: from short seconds of eye contact with a stranger or a known other person to intense relationships where there might be moments that feel as if both were one and the same person. Twosomeness occurs in many places. It could be one's love-life or at work. Twosomeness—or the meeting—is one of the first things we experience: the meeting with the mother or the person in her place. In the vast majority of cases, and when things go well, the meeting of mother and child can be compared with a pair of lovers (Stern, 1991). Only couples in love look each other in the eyes for as long as a mother and a newborn baby. As we saw in Chapter Three, this meeting and its intensity are crucial for the developments that will follow. In rapid succession after this, the infant meets with the others: the family, and the group, whether it is large or small. These first meetings and the way they develop are fundamental from a psychological point of view, as the basis for all future meetings.

Later on, we enter into many "meetings" and couple relationships: playmates, friends, and a girlfriend; the childhood sweetheart; the teenage sweetheart; classmates at school and college with whom we work out assignments; the work-mate; colleagues. Some we choose ourselves, and some are chosen for us. We are given roles and we take up roles in these two-person relationships. We are conscious of some and unconscious of others. We gather experience and learn from each and every meeting. Each meeting leaves traces and becomes part of what we bring with us to the next meeting. Some experiences and traces become more determinative than others. We cannot survive without other people—the other—when an assignment must be carried out or life must be lived. We cannot always avoid the others. Life can be difficult with them, but it can also be difficult without them. André Gorz's last book is a love-letter to his wife, and in it he writes, "You offered me access to a dimension of supplementary otherness" (Gorz, 2008, p. 10). Perhaps this expresses the longing or the hope we have for the meeting with the other, both in our love-life and our working lives. A meeting with something that supplements ourselves is the foundation for being able to achieve more than one person can alone. This supplement can fulfil desires and ambitions. It makes synergy and fruitfulness possible. Another longing associated with meeting can be the elimination of the feeling of loneliness. Knowing that at least one other person will be there if one is forsaken. Being forsaken is bound up with anxiety—no one can manage completely alone. Perhaps because of these great and fundamental hopes and longings, there are often great expectations of a couple in love or colleagues at work.

Psychodynamic theory is just as overwhelmingly diverse in this field as in the fields of personality and development psychology. This is because "established psychoanalysis" thinks in individual terms within its original framework of understanding. It is the individual who has the difficulty—or symptom—in the individual's uncompleted personality development, and, therefore, the solution must also be found in the individual. If a couple has problems, the solution, in the traditional view, must be that both of them go for analysis, but individually (Jensen & Hejl, 1987; Olsen, 2002). Another argument against having the couple coming for treatment together is that the complexity in the transference and countertransference pattern will increase to an unmanageable level and, consequently, weaken the validity of the analysis.

As explained in Chapter Three, psychodynamic theory has developed over time to understand relationships as the source of both difficulties and delights. The psychodynamic hypothesis that all development occurs in relationships is well documented. The theoretical understanding of a working pair draws some of its theory from the love relationship and some more generally from theories on management. In psychodynamic coaching, the starting point for understanding will be that the individual, as mentioned in earlier chapters, has fixations, personal patterns, and compulsive repetitions to a major or minor degree. How, or to what extent, these patterns come decisively into play is especially influenced by the important and regular relationships and systems in which the individual is included. A couple, whether they are lovers or a pair at work, are in just such a regular and important relationship. It could be said that the relationship and the system are the developing fluid in which patterns, fantasies, and emotions are made visible. This is also an everyday experience for most people: when planning to make a speech, it is not insignificant *where* it is to be made and *who* is in the audience. One's parents? The boss? One's lover? Journalists? The ex-wife? A competitor?

Psychodynamic coaching is not concerned with investigating the client's fundamental conflict and going from there to healing. That is not the aim with couples, either. It is not the two in the couple—the clients' fundamental conflicts individually—that are in focus. We know that the personal fixations exist, and that they play a decisive part. In the psychodynamic coaching of a couple, we are concerned with *how* it interacts and is played out in the present, and how to set up a realistic and desirable future for the couple, whether they are to continue as a couple or whether it means that they will go their separate ways.

Psychodynamic coaching for couples is especially inspired by the theoretical understandings that arose in the 1970s, when there were developments in the synthesis of system theory and psychoanalysis. General system theory is a theory about the ability of systems to find a balance—homeostasis. This is the study of the organization of complex systems, internal connections, energy, process, and structure. The system is built up from the participating members' mutual relationships, and the centre of interest is more the communication and behaviour and the way they affect the system than the processes in the individual. If changes are to be achieved in a system, the existing homeostasis must be broken down, that is, relationships, boundaries, and rules must be broken down. A social system is understood to function according to the same principles as a biological system. The system maintains its homeostasis by circular causality. This means that the system supplies self-referring stimuli and feedback that reinforce each other. American psychoanalysts who have been more orientated towards the psychology of the ego (cf. Chapter Three, the section about Erikson) have attempted to link this part of psychoanalytical understanding with system theoretical understanding. Wile's model is an example of this type of understanding. It appeared in connection with clinical work, and, therefore, terms like *therapist* and *treatment* are used.

Wile (quoted from Jensen & Hejl, 1987) assumes as his starting point that each of the partners has an individual position that is concerned with thoughts and feelings, processes, conclusions, and behaviour in connection with the other. As a result of this, the partners have an over-sensitivity that, under pressure, leads them to react as they do. The couple's problems are understood as negative interplay between these over-sensitivities. Here, a position is to be understood as a present psychological state that is a consequence of the interaction of the personality with the current psychological situation. In other words, the states and actions produced by the ego. The over-sensitive reaction of one triggers the over-sensitive reaction of the other. As an example, one might be afraid of conflicts, and pull in his horns at the slightest indication of a disagreement. The other is nervous and insecure about ambiguity, and tries to create clarity by increasingly asking questions, speaking clearly and pressing the point. This reinforces the partner's over-sensitivity to conflicts, resulting in further withdrawal, which, in turn, reinforces the over-sensitivity to ambiguity. Their patterns reinforce each other mutually, bringing increasing frustration, which again wears down the advantages created by the hopes and feelings associated with the relationship. It can be said that they are each other's stimuli in relation to constraints and patterns, and this is the essence of their mutual negative binding. Wile (quoted from Jensen & Hejl, 1987) proposed a treatment strategy that matches this understanding. First, the two positions must be made clear, and then the inner workings of this interplay must be revealed. It requires skill and sensitivity in the therapist to arrange this process so that the revelation occurs at the same time, since each partner might be afraid that the therapist is taking sides with the other.

In Europe, work was done in the same period—the 1970s and 1980s—to link psychoanalysis with system theory. In the UK, in the Tavistock tradition, and in Germany there were parallel developments of clinical methods and theoretical understanding that formed the background for the understanding on which psychodynamic couple and family therapy is based today. In the mid 1950s, the anthropologist Bateson, leader of the Palo-Alto group (later the Milan school), developed the system theory which is integrated in many ways into psychodynamic thought, and in this way the psychodynamic system theory was formed (Olsen, 2002; Visholm, 2004). Thus, system theory was "extended" with the extra dimension of the concept of "the unconscious" and the whole area of psychodynamic development psychology. It is also the unconscious stimuli and the silent, unconscious communication, thoughts, fantasies, and the logic of feelings that are included in the understanding of the complex interplay of the system and, thereby, in the interplay of the system with its surroundings. Psychoanalytical theory, primarily in the form of object relation theory, which claims that all personal development occurs in interplay with others, linked with system theory, forms the basis for psychodynamic coaching of couples. A couple is seen as a system—an entity—in which the relationship is understood, among other things, through the concept of projective identification. In this way, the couple is the system in which the problems, if any, arise, and it is also the system where "healing" can occur. It means that the transference and countertransference relationships become manageable to work with, since the internal psychological processes in the individual and the interaction between the two partners can be seen and understood as connected, and in reciprocal exchanges with each other. It can be regarded as an unconscious communication that goes on between the partners. In this way, a possible framework is provided for interpretation.

The following is a description of essential theoretical understandings of the couple and their interaction. The partners meet and project their own fantasies into the other. In this way, each creates an internal image of the other. If the couple are lovers, then one could say that we do not fall in love so much with the other as with the *conception* of the other. If it is a couple of partners at work, we would probably formulate it to say that we place our hopes, ambitions, and expectations in the conception of the other. Of course, the partners can and do have different and more realistic data about each other, and these are woven into the conception. There is an extremely important difference between a pair of lovers and a pair of work partners. The lovers have a unique source of energy in the fact of being in love, where very little room is left for worries. A pair of working partners—in most cases— will have arisen from a more prosaic constellation, and for that reason more often includes realistically based worries and fears. However, a couple of working partners might be formed in a context that can be compared with falling in love, or, as it is frequently formulated, "on their honeymoon". These conceptions under the spell of love can be very strong, and appear absolutely real to the partners: think how a young person reacts if someone older makes the slightest criticism of the chosen boy or girlfriend, or how a couple starting out in business can defend each other and their idea, regardless of any facts, for instance relating to the market situation. It might be very difficult to admit any other points of view.

As outlined in Chapter Three, we go through certain crucial periods in our development that are created in, and characteristic of, the relationships we have been in and are still in. The course taken by these relationships forms the background psychologically for later relationships we might enter into. The early object relationships with the mother are embedded in our unconscious, just like the Oedipal relationships. The Oedipal relationships are associated with attachment, "the progress of the love affair" with the parent of the opposite sex, and, at the same time, it is the first important experience of having a rival. It is, therefore, the first relationship where we experience that there is also a risk associated with strong emotional relationships. Relationships with siblings form part of the basis of what we carry with us of conscious and unconscious traces in connection with jealousy and envy. In these relationships, we have learnt quite a lot about competition, collaboration, solidarity, and the field of tension between hate and love. Many of the experiences we have—or do not have— from our childhood, with or without siblings, play an essential role when we work in pairs or in groups and/or are assigned management functions. Our way of functioning as colleagues is often based on emotional traces from the sibling group (Huffington & Miller, 2008). It could be said that each member of a couple has met external relationships in the course of development, and been through courses of events where these figures have been internalized as a basis for inner relationships with authorities and colleagues. This forms the background for how the individual "plays his cards"—that is, how the inner relationships become "co-players" in the outer relationships. We help to "direct our own plot".

In the couple relationship between the couple at work and perhaps especially in the love relationship, we seek to correct or compensate for the relationship with our parents, which formed the parts of our personality that we want to change; we repeat our patterns, now hoping for a different result from the original one. A couple, therefore, consists of two people, each with their own patterns, together with the mutual third, the relationship itself, that is, the specific way in which the interplay works out, especially through projective identification. The factors on which attention is particularly centred in the couple relationship, both in the case of love and the working relationship, are boundaries with regard to each other and the world in general, rules: what actions are legitimate, and what is prohibited? Power and authority—who decides the rules and makes the decisions? And roles: who does what, psychologically as well as practically, to make it all work? Communications between the partners, both conscious and unconscious, are what create and maintain the situation described above, and it is also through communications that changes can be made (Jensen & Hejl, 1987; Olsen, 2002).

In gestalt psychology, which is an independent psychodynamic school of thought, different typologies of communication patterns have been described, which can be inspiring on closer study (Berne, 1967; James & Jongeward, 1976; Perls, 1973). They can be criticized as somewhat simplified, "ego" orientated and stereotypical, and, thus, liable to overlook the complexity and refinement in the communication of a couple, each with their own unique history and personality. Every couple—exactly like each individual—has a unique common history, which, as time passes, will increasingly become a significant part of the relations. In psychodynamic coaching, this means that, for instance, when a manager asks for advice because there are management problems between herself and her co-manager, then the coach must, as a minimum, think of "them"—the management couple—as an entity, of which only one part might be present. However, it might also be relevant to suggest that the other—the co-manager—should also join in the coaching. It is a precondition that the co-manager can also see that there is a problem in the relationship, which they must do something about. This cannot always be taken for granted; it is quite common for management couples as well as for lovers to feel that the other is the problem, and that the solution must be for him or her to "work things out" so that the relationship works properly again. Nevertheless, it is seen to an increasing degree that the partners come together and that there is a common understanding that "we" have a problem, which both of us are part of, and, therefore, we are both part of the solution.

When seeking to understand the dynamics of the couple, a central concept is collusion, which means unconscious interplay between two or more (Dicks, 1967; Jakobsen & Visholm, 1987; Olsen, 2002; Willi, 1984). This concept was developed with the couple of lovers in focus, but there are obvious possibilities for understanding it in connection with the couple at work. The skeleton of the theory is that the partners (in a couple) are fixed in the same phase of development, and that their unconscious collusion is connected with it. The different phases of development considered here are the classic phases from Freudian developmental psychology: the oral phase, the anal phase, and the Oedipal phase. In addition, Willi supplements them with an unconscious narcissistic collusion, which is of interest when we are investigating couples in management, because management often attracts people with narcissistic needs, since it is an organizational position that provides considerable attention and focus. Thus, unconscious collusion is the expression that the partners have the same unconscious themes, which they are drawn towards working with. They might, for instance, be themes about caring, autonomy, identity, authority, and strength. These are central in both a love relationship and in a work-related partnership. The parties have the same theme, but it manifests itself differently.

The caring theme can appear either as the need to give or to receive care. There is a plus and a minus variant of every theme.

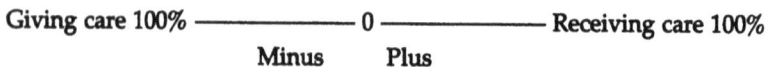

Giving care 100% ——————— 0 ——————— Receiving care 100%
                          Minus   Plus

Here, the theme—or parameter—is care. On the right is a scale for receiving care, and on the left is a scale for giving care. The partners are out at the extreme points, one at each end of the scale, with one giving and the other receiving care. For shorter or longer periods, they might fit together well, but at some stage both partners—though not necessarily at the same time—will tire of their polarized positions. It happens most frequently when a couple's balance is challenged by external circumstances. In the case of lovers, it might happen when one becomes unemployed, or loses parents, or when the couple has a baby, when one becomes seriously ill, or when one is extremely successful. For the couple at work, the balance of the system might be upset in connection with reorganization, a merger, cutbacks, altered assignments, changes in production, new technology, new managers or owners, or success coming from outside. For example, success may shift the balance for a couple where one becomes the main figure in a television broadcast. That partner received so much positive attention in the broadcast that the other partner's envy flared up, with consequences for their emotional relationship. What felt right and good earlier on can become constrictive and narrow. The role can become like a jacket that is too small. The interpretation of unconscious collusion is that the partners have organized their resistance to accepting that each needs to receive as well as give care, by only taking on one side. One has a point of view that can be stated simply as: "I am big and strong, can cope with everything and do not need help and comfort". Resistance to this drives him or her right out to the left of the scale. The other's point of view can similarly be stated simply as: "I am small and weak, cannot do anything without support, help, and comforting", which means resistance to seeing his or her own strength and possibilities, so he or she will be driven from inside to the right-hand end of the scale. Both partners will be wearied by these extreme positions, and, in the long run, they prove unsatisfactory. Here, as in other situations, resistance will only temporarily maintain a satisfactory state. Where originally they were fascinated by the way they supplemented each other so well, each will later see the other as a constraint. The provider of care might feel: "I am so tired of the way it all depends on me. I am always the one who has to take care of everything. I simply do not have the strength—I must get out of this relationship". The one who is cared for might feel: "I'm being suffocated. I never have any say in what we do—everything is fixed or decided beforehand, and whatever I do, it is not good enough, not fast enough—I must get out of this relationship".

The way it manifests itself varies, but resistance is concerned with the same thing. The polarization that previously functioned well has become destructive. The unconscious collusion theory is very practically orientated. In psychodynamic coaching for a couple, it can facilitate the process if there is a slight element of "teaching", that is, a didactic explanation of a concept, so that the clients and coach together can investigate the couple's unconscious collusive relationship. The coach might, through the work of uncovering and understanding, form a hypothesis about the couple's unconscious collusion, which can then be passed on to the couple, so that the work can continue from there. The more data that can be provided—observations and specific illustrations from coaching process—the better. In most cases, it will be understood at the cognitive level that everyone needs both to receive and to give care.

Understanding is a good starting point for the work on the emotions that is to follow. Understanding often creates the legitimacy in investigative work. If the "discovery" is to lead to acknowledgement, it is necessary to investigate which emotions and complex states are in play when the resistance pattern is repeated in the specific day-to-day situations. Even though the partners want to come out of the destructive state, as a rule there will also be psychological forces whose purpose is to retain them in the original balance. It wants the quality of familiarity in the repetitive pattern. The couple will also be subject to ambivalence, and, on the one hand, wish for the change, while at the unconscious level they do not want it. It applies to couples as to individuals that it facilitates the necessary change if the partners have ego strength. Working to achieve development calls for an ability to tolerate frustration, both in individuals and in couples. Unlike individuals, the task for the couple involves an additional mutual dependency, which can increase the frustration. The current emotional state of the couple is also significant for how the coaching will progress and to what extent it will lead to a positive result. If the relationship is strongly competitive, it makes the work more difficult. What is unlucky for one will please the other. Conversely, if the relationship is characterized by collaboration, meaning that the partners agree that there could be a positive element in their conflict, and can see that negative feelings are also an expression of emotional interest, then it will support the task of coaching.

Delegation (Jakobsen & Visholm, 1987; Scharff & Scharff, 1987; Visholm, 1993) is another useful concept in the understanding of what dynamics might be active under the surface of the relationship between a couple. Delegation is connected with the phenomenon that one of the partners might unconsciously delegate to the other psychological assignments that he or she has not been able to "solve". This happens through projective identification processes. These delegations might come from different parts of the personality. Delegation from the ego might be associated with unfulfilled ambitions, while delegations from the superego might be concerned with guilt and making amends for earlier actions, while id delegations might be associated with "living out" forbidden pleasurable or destructive sides. One partner's subconscious is, thus, asking the other partner to do something that cannot be integrated into the first partner's own personality. We also know the expression in daily use about a person achieving ambitions through someone else. It is typically used about children who live up to their parents' unstated ambitions of raising the whole family up the social ladder, or about the wife who becomes "a special person" through her husband's achievements.

Management positions are often attractive to people who seek narcissistic gratification, because there are multiple chances of mirroring in these positions, not to mention power, importance, and attention. It is, therefore, important for managers to possess what Kernberg (1978, 1984, 1994, 1998) called "healthy narcissism", which means the ability to stand out and receive acclaim or admiration, even be idolized, *without* being disturbed, or, in other words, to keep one's feet on the ground and maintain contact with true reality. A manager's unrealistic and enlarged self-image, with no basis in reality, can be the ruin of an organization.

"Regression to narcissism is a permanent danger for leaders, the more so as their followers find themselves uplifted by their leader's narcissism and collude with it" (Hirschhorn, 1999, p. 142). Narcissistic collusion can arise between a manager and the employees, but can also arise and be maintained between two partners working as a pair of managers. It can be difficult for the rest of the organization to break through the way they are narcissistically "in love" with their own mirror images.

A pair of managers of this type were "sent" for coaching. They had a resistance to seeing reality as it was, and the way they worked as a pair was characterized by a narcissistic collusion. *She* had difficulty in recognizing her own competencies and qualities. She held her insights and knowledge back. Her severe superego would not allow her to believe in her own worth; she had learnt as a child that women are not clever, and under no circumstances should they draw attention to themselves. But she could always praise and acknowledge others. *He* had a serious narcissistic disturbance, and, in order to maintain his distorted self-image, he needed stimulation from others. Unconsciously, they associated themselves with each other. She idolized him, associated herself symbiotically with him, and could thus become a part of something better, which temporarily repaired her low self-esteem and self-confidence. He then had a mirror that told him: "You are the most handsome and the wisest person on this earth", which temporarily eased his inner pain.

They were referred for coaching by the senior executives above them. The economy had been untenable for some time; there were conflicts in all staff groups, and in the management group at the same level as this couple there was dissatisfaction with the strategic collaboration. All remarks in the nature of complaints were ignored. Minor grumbles or attempts to get help with problems in the staff groups were overheard, devalued, or referred back with the comment that: "Everything is going fine, so you can easily sort that out yourselves." At more or less public appearances in the organization, the two of them always praised each other, almost flirting with their relationship and their joint excellence. They did not do it with sexual undertones, but in a blind, idealizing manner. It was not until the senior management approached them personally in connection with mass dismissals and numerous vacant positions that the glass bubble finally burst: they risked being dismissed themselves if they did not get the department on an even keel again within four months. They were given an ultimatum: either they must take part in coaching or they must resign. They chose coaching.

Now, it would be possible to conduct a lengthy discussion on whether it is possible to work with psychodynamic coaching at all under those conditions. It is always problematical when developments are forced through under pressure. On the other hand, it is difficult to imagine that any couple with a narcissistic disturbance would seek help on their own initiative. There are two tasks in this situation. The first is linked to the authority in the organizational system, to clarify one's terms and requirements, and then confront the couple with them and with the real situation. The other task is the task of development—coaching. The first task must be performed by the senior executives, and the second by the coach, together with the couple. It is important not to mix the aspect of power into the coaching process. First of all, a third of the course was spent on securing the framework the couple had with them, that is, fending off all denials and ideas that the faults were to be found everywhere else, and creating an insight into the fact that it was a defence against the harsh reality that they had not much control over anything. They had to focus on the extent of the problem and concentrate on the fact that they themselves were actually the ones who had a problem, and needed to work out a solution. It succeeded. The next third of the course was focused on their relationship, and the final third was concerned with how any future collaboration was to be established.

It happens sometimes that psychodynamic coaching does not succeed, and it is not possible to break down or minimize the defence. This might mean that the course has to be stopped. A narcissistic collusion might be difficult to work with and require therapy instead of coaching, because early damage is involved, and the goal is more like healing. It is quite crucial that the coach has the education and training to assess this and refer the clients on if necessary.

During the investigation and clarification of the relationship of the couple described, many emotions were uncovered, and it became clear that the context was full of competition and rivalry. It went from idealization to devaluation; from seeing the other as the perfect partner to seeing the other as the worst partner, who was to blame for all their troubles. The devaluation phase led into an "awaking" to reality—"we are both part of this"—to an overwhelming sense of being incapable of making decisions because the task of restoring proper functionality both in production and in relationships in the department felt insurmountable. The couple set up agreements with other staff in the organization to support them in their future management, both of finances and human resources. In a transitional period, a financial specialist was appointed to the management and the staff group were given training in collaboration together with their management.

Case: Bridget and Howard

Below is a more detailed example of a course of psychodynamic coaching for a management couple. This course is more "ordinary" and normal, and can, therefore, serve as an illustrative example. The description of the coaching follows the same structure as in personal individual psychodynamic coaching.

1. The client's first contact.
2. The first coaching session: objectives and framework.
3. The course of coaching.
4. Conclusion: evaluation and leave-taking.

The client's contact

The enquiry was a telephone call. A woman introduced herself briefly, giving her name, and then she asked, "Do you do couple therapy for managers? I think that is probably what we need." I did not manage to say anything at all, and her voice came through as brusque and slightly ironic. I wanted to say no. However, I introduced myself, and said, "It is a bit difficult to answer that. Could you please tell me some more about what you are looking for?" I felt her voice seemed to change. She sounded warmer and less offensive. She explained that she and her masculine co-manager had difficulty in working in harmony, and with getting the department to function smoothly. Some of the staff complained about him to her. She could describe him as slightly introverted and herself as more outgoing. "He might seem grumpy, but he isn't. That is what I have told my girls." I noticed that I felt she was talking about him as if he were her husband, and that she referred to "my girls" several times: associations with family relationships. But that was, in fact, what she had said at the beginning: couple therapy. She explained that they had agreed that something had to be done, and they would like to make an appointment. We booked an appointment, and there was no great problem in finding a time that suited everyone.

My immediate impression after the conversation was that she was controlling it. I had not asked for anything like enough details. It sounded as if she knew what the problem was and what should be done about it. I should have asked about the organization and how the problems showed up. But I "swallowed" the information she fed me uncritically. I felt like an implement that just had to lever that agreement into place, and then move on to the next. In fact, I felt a little foolish. Or perhaps used.

As described in the chapter on individual coaching, I took care here, too, to write down whatever thoughts and feelings came to me, and my associations on this first contact. The themes of control, being overlooked, and feeling exploited were later to prove to be central ones. There are valuable data in feelings of countertransference.

The first coaching session: objectives and framework

The time came for the first session, and the two appeared. They gave a well-maintained, modern impression. Their introduction was polite and slightly nervous. Bridget, aged fifty-three, had been a nurse since she completed her training at the age of twenty-five. She had held leading positions for twenty-one years, as ward sister, senior staff nurse, and now as head nurse. Howard was forty-seven, had risen rapidly to consultant, and written his doctoral thesis at the age of forty-three. He described how he actively took part in professional associations nationally and internationally, and had received several awards and grants. This was his first management position, where he was the senior consultant. Howard and Bridget formed the management at a medical centre, with several somatic departments under it. Bridget had worked in these departments for fifteen years, while Howard had been appointed as senior consultant three years ago, when the new centre structure was set up. Howard was actually appointed in connection with the reorganization, where, at the same time, the form of management was changed from a single-line medical management to joint centre management. This meant that where previously the consultant had taken the decisions, if he and the matron did not agree, they now ranked equally, and had to reach the same decisions. The partially new hospital management, which was the management level above the centre management, had announced a series of values as guiding principles for management, including consensus and dialogue. Against that background, Howard and Bridget decided to reserve one day each week for their management work. This was when matters were to be discussed and decisions made.

The meetings worked very well at first. The couple got to know each other and enjoyed their shared ambitions for the department. However, after a time, some meetings were not held, and Bridget noticed that it was almost always Howard who cancelled them. Bridget was the one who did the talking. Howard seemed a little distant. Bridget said, "Well, now it is not working properly, and we need couple therapy, so where are you going to start, Ulla?" I noted that Bridget's directing attitude irritated me, and my spontaneous impulse was to say, "Now, now, hold your horses! I am the one who decides things here." My next thought was that it might just be nervousness and eagerness to get started. Instead of confronting her, I said, "Well, I would like to start with each of you describing your own difficulties and your common difficulties. How you experience them and how it affects you, what feelings they arouse and how you understand them, in other words, why do you think you feel the way you do?", and I continued, "I suggest that Howard should begin, since I have not heard so much from you, Howard." I registered that my impulse had some consequence after all: I took control and managed to stop Bridget temporarily. It could be considered an adequate action, but it was also undeniably a kind of reprimand. Bridget smiled and replied, "That's a good idea, because I am so communicative!" "Hm. One-nil to Bridget," I thought. I was getting thoroughly entangled in a sort of rivalry.

Howard took over and began his description. He had arrived three years ago full of expectations and had been looking forward to the job. The departments in the area were respected and well reputed, and expectations of the new centre management construction were positive. He had been there earlier as a junior doctor, and met Bridget, who, at that time, had been the new matron. He remembered her as open, friendly to the staff, and professionally deeply committed. That impression had been confirmed at the job interview. He thought things went very well at the start. They had held regular meetings, discussed the way they divided the work, their ambitions for the department, the staff, and their mutual relationship. They allocated their contact with the hospital management according to which subject was involved, with Bridget dealing with everything concerned with nursing and Howard taking charge of medical matters. When it was financial business, they had dealt with it jointly whenever it was practically possible. As part of the division of the work, he was to take charge of the "outgoing" professional contact. This meant drawing in projects and funds, finding the best doctors for the department, and representing the department in professional connections inland and abroad. Bridget was to keep him continually informed on internal matters.

The more he had taken care of his assignments, the more he felt he was moving further away from the department, not only physically, but also mentally. He had often been unable to attend the management meetings, and he had, to a greater and greater extent, been informed by Bridget about things that had happened, and what decisions she had already taken. She had not told him what was actually going on, so that he could have any influence on it. At joint meetings with the staff, and once or twice at the morning meeting, he had felt that he had been overruled by Bridget in public, because she had not informed him until then of matters that made a critical difference to what he had just said. His countermove had been to withdraw and shut himself out. He thought he had got a completely wrong impression of Bridget. She was more loyal to "her girls" and "her department", and used him as whipping boy. In all the time he had been employed there, he had never heard a single word of recognition for all the funds and all the positive PR he had created for the department, not even when they had been voted "Department of the Year", which was entirely due to his efforts in maintaining networks, positive lobbying, and getting two international research projects set up. For some time now, he had been considering moving away.

Bridget could confirm the earlier part of the story, about the beginning of their management collaboration, their agreements about dividing assignments and two-way communications. She had increasingly felt abandoned, left alone, and sometimes left in the lurch with difficult situations concerned with budget affairs and disagreements with the staff. Just as soon as there was the slightest hint of conflict, Howard would disappear, and she had had to manage everything alone. There had not been time to pass on information. Howard had not answered e-mails and had not answered his mobile phone. So, she had gradually stopped contacting him, and decided that she would have to deal with things herself. At any rate, the department and the staff were not going to suffer because he let them down. She was angry and tired, and did not remember that Howard had ever contacted her either to ask about how things were going or how she was getting on. She tried to prime him when he had to take part in the hospital management, but it was necessary to be able to get hold of him. She could confirm that there had been some embarrassing scenes when he had revealed his lack of interest and knowledge about the department in common forums. She felt that she had been totally excluded from the professional work and had become a "high level service person". I asked them whether there had ever been any complaints about their management or their results. Bridget answered, "No. Seen from the outside, everything is running perfectly. It is just us who are suffering under it." Howard confirmed this.

I did not intervene, but moved on to the next point: "What is going to be the goal for this course of coaching?"

Bridget said, "Well, either we must get to love each other again, or we will have to separate." Howard said nothing. I asked, "Could it work out with anything less? Do you have to love each other?" Howard said, "I don't think so—what I mean is that we have to go in for this passionately, or else it won't work. I have always loved my job." Bridget said, "I have always really liked my job. But love is for the people in my private life. I feel it is an admission of failure if it is your work that you love." Howard shook his head with his eyes half closed and raised to the ceiling, as if to signal that Bridget was beyond the pale.

During the session, it became obvious that they both felt let down and forsaken. Their defence took the form of self-justification. They had the same dream about their work, but for different reasons. Their approaches to work and the workplace were fundamentally different. Bridget was more attached to the workplace and the staff than to the work, while Howard was the complete opposite. Both were eager to do something useful, and both wanted to be valued by their staff, but in different ways. Both had ambitions for the department and for themselves.

What had started as a collaboration full of hope had so far ended as a contest for each other's, the staff's, and the rest of the world's admiration. The objective for the coaching was formulated as to investigate why they had ended up in this state, and whether there was any basis for continuing their collaboration. The agreed framework was ten sessions of two hours each, two each month for the first three months, and then one session per month. They commented that they had expected that it could be cleared up faster.

The course of coaching

The course of coaching fell into several sections. Each session started with half an hour of recounting and reflecting ongoing events that were relevant to the coaching procedure, but only half an hour. In accordance with the goal for psychodynamic coaching, the investigative task was to find the connection between past and present in order to understand the underlying dynamics in the present relationship that was being enacted between the two of them. When the work of looking at their individual stories and their significance for the present was completed, it would form the basis for working on the future, regardless of whether they would remain together or not. Therefore, the first part of the process had a historical focus.

When the coaching involves a couple, there are two individual stories as well as the shared common one—the relationship and its story. The common story can be told from the two individual points of view, and their perspectives. The problem that has been presented must be formulated, and the investigative work can begin. They agreed that the problem was that they both felt let down and left alone with very large assignments. They felt that they were drawing further and further apart from each other, which was unfortunate and unproductive, both with regard to the tasks of the centre and the well-being of the staff.

It might be necessary for the coach to take an active part in formulating the joint problem, because the partners might have a resistance to the idea that they have anything in common. This was not the case with Bridget and Howard, because they had "come in time"; that is, before their difficulties had become a conflict. To begin the work with their individual stories, I asked them each to draw nine scenes from their lives. There were to be three from childhood, two from when they were growing up, two from their adult private lives, and two from their working life, one from before the present situation and one from the present situation. (See Appendix 4.) This task can also be used in individual coaching, but it is especially suitable when there is more than one client, because some of the work is done outside the actual sessions. Of course, a drawing also means that the process around the personal history becomes less exploratory and detailed. Coaching couples is also primarily concerned with what is happening *between* the two, and thus their personal history plays a less prominent role. Bridget and Howard brought their drawings with them, and at first were a little shy about showing them. Bridget went first. She told her story without interruptions. Next, Howard was allowed to ask about factual matters—with the aim of becoming better informed, not to discuss anything. After Howard's questions, I had a few about factual matters myself. Then I asked Howard to make contact with everything he had thought, felt, and found associations with in connection with Bridget's drawings and narrative. With as little censorship as possible, he had to try to put across to Bridget what happened inside him as he saw and heard her account. Afterwards we repeated the process, now with Howard, his drawings, and his story.

The main impression from Bridget's drawings was how active she was in all the pictures. She was the older sibling to a younger brother and sister. Her mother was divorced, a single parent with a demanding job as a lawyer. Bridget was her mother's helper and the one who guaranteed that their family life functioned. She had a problematical relationship with her mother, and felt her mother failed them. She was often angry, and one drawing showed a scene where Bridget was having a violent argument with her mother. It was not until much later in her own career that she understood her mother's dilemma as a single provider. She had been—as she put it—kind and unkind in equal amounts to her brother and sister. She acted as a mother to them and decided things, but she also helped them with homework and lunchpacks, comforted them if anyone had annoyed them at school, and so on. In all Bridget's drawings she was faceless. When asked about how she felt and what feelings she had, Bridget became quite upset. She explained that there had not been time to take any notice of that. "So nobody else did, either," she added. The logic of the feelings was that if nobody was interested in how she felt, then there was no point in showing it on her face. Perhaps Bridget had not always been in contact with her feelings either, because it was too painful. She still did not show how she was feeling, but had forgotten that now—in contrast to her impressions or experience as a child—there might be someone who actually was interested.

Bridget had also drawn a scene from a Saturday evening. Those were the good evenings: her mother was home, the house was clean, they had eaten and washed up, and afterwards they had a cosy time with Saturday sweets. These were really occasions she remembered as glowingly happy. She added, "I promised myself that my children would often have times like that." There was a longish period when Bridget's mother had a partner whom Bridget did not like, and the Saturday evenings were spoilt. "He stole our cosy times together. My younger brother and sister liked him, and he was much nicer to them than to me. I thought he exploited my mother, and he never joined in anything, or helped her, either with work or with money. It ended with a big row, of course, and he was thrown out." The drawings from her present working life—from the current situation—had many points that were similar to the Saturday evening scene.

In Howard's drawings of his childhood there was a lot of community spirit. The family were drawn together, holding each other's hands and looking happy. He had grown up in the country, and everyone joined in the work except him. He had drawn himself as a very thin little boy sitting bent over his books, while the others—his brothers and sisters and friends—were outdoors. They were playing. Everyone was happy. There was a scene from the time he qualified for university, and from when he took the Hippocratic Oath. His parents were there on both occasions, and were clearly very proud; it radiated from them. Howard was the first and only academic in his family. His grandfather was a farmer, and an uncle had taken over the farm from the grandfather. Howard's father was an electrician and was studying further to qualify for certification, when his brother, Howard's uncle, became seriously ill and could no longer run the farm. Howard's father gave up his further training and took over the farm, which he ran together with Howard's mother, who was a nurse. She worked in the home care service at the same time, because they needed the money. Howard's father had dreamed of being an engineer when he completed his electrical studies, but had to abandon the dream.

Howard proved to be bright and good at his schoolwork, especially at mathematics. His father supported him and helped with homework. He said that, looking back, he thought he must have been irritating at times to his siblings, because he was often "let off" duties and from helping in the work with the animals on the farm, or at harvest, etc., because he had to be allowed to study in peace. He could not remember them being angry. It was as if the mission that had been given to Howard did not come only from his father and the abandoned dream, but was supported by the whole family. It was a strong mission from the whole family that "someone" had to make up for the misfortune they had suffered, that, through a sense of responsibility, Howard's father had given up his own ambitions for an education to take over the family farm. That "someone" was Howard. The choice of study and profession was probably not entirely left to chance, either, since in the family's view it was even better to be a doctor than an engineer, and there might be an unconscious fantasy that with a doctor in the family the story of disease would not be repeated.

The original family were shown in the drawing of his adult private life, too. They were holding hands there as well, and he said that they probably saw the family most in their spare time. After questions, reflections, and associations, primarily from Bridget and myself, Bridget was asked to describe what associations she saw between Howard's story and the present situation. In the same way, Howard was asked to describe connections between Bridget's story and the present situation. Both Bridget and Howard were really good at seeing connections and formulating hypotheses. Bridget could not imagine that she might not be responsible for everything, and responsible for finishing off whatever the others had left undone. She could not see it as a possibility that one can get help by asking for it, or the possibility of obtaining a positive result from reprimanding anyone who had not done something that was really their duty. She had not learnt that things could be otherwise, and, without reflection, had transferred the conditions of her childhood to adult life.

Howard had difficulty in understanding that it could be a problem that he threw himself "blindly" into his own tasks, without noticing joint ones. "There are others to do those after all." He had never known any other situation. He wondered why nobody clapped or said hurray when he earned "good grades" for the department—he was surprised at being met with grumpiness and envy instead.

The very fact that these connections are put into words helps the work to progress, but also hearing the other partner understand, take in, and be concerned with one's own story and the joint situation has an emotional effect that brings relief. It does not remove the differences, but it paves the way for containing and integration. Both drawings of their situation at work before it began to get difficult showed the pleasure of expectation. Howard's drawing showed happy smiley faces and Bridget's had a shooting star.

At this stage in the coaching, they were asked to tell their joint story. Both started in the same way, with great expectations and high hopes. After that, they especially noted different episodes. Bridget had noticed occasions when she had felt alone with all the tidying up, feeling deserted and having no idea of what she could do other than simply getting on with it. "There I was again with the washing up, and the little ones were out playing," as she put it. Howard had chiefly noted situations where he had been prevented from doing things or disturbed before he completed tasks, or where the congratulations he expected did not materialize. He had never discussed them with Bridget. "Never go back to a damp squib," he almost chanted, laconically. Bridget and Howard both looked into which feelings and impressions they had had of each other's motives along the way, and, among other things, in which ways these were embedded in their story.

I contributed along the way with data from some of the feelings, associations, and countertransferences that had been among the things I registered as we went along. One example was my urge to rival Bridget about who was steering the coaching process. This had given me an insight into another aspect of her responsibility, which was the need to be in control. I also drew attention to the urge I felt to protect and encourage Howard, who presented himself as a somewhat delicate person physically, who needed undisturbed freedom from other tasks to do his own work, and the hypothesis about the mission he had been assigned from home. Bridget could recognize the feeling that Howard was someone who needed to be protected. She had not thought about it before, but could see that it strengthened her need to "carry the responsibility". Howard thought the hypothesis about the "mission" was difficult. He found it hard to accept that the decision to become a doctor was not his own fully conscious decision, made independently of the family. On the other hand, he could reflect on the freedom from inner pressure it would give him if he did *not* constantly have to work at being the leader in his field. Now he had to reconsider what he *himself* wanted to do with his working life. The part of the hypothesis he could understand was that he should become a doctor in order to take care of the family, and make sure they did not suffer any accidents. His family consulted him about all sorts of things, and he often wondered whether he should send them away, because one should not be a doctor to one's own family. He had once told his sister to go to her own doctor. A short time later, his mother was on the phone, and thought it was really something he could deal with. "And so I did after all," he said, with a wry smile.

The next part of the coaching process was concerned with creating an awareness that, from a psychological point of view, they were no longer children, or bound by the feelings that were linked to earlier situations, but that now—having become aware of these patterns—could form their lives and relationships themselves, based on their own wishes, as appropriate for their age and situations. I asked them to work on the following questions: What do you want yourself? What do you want from your co-manager? What do you think will be your co-manager's opinion about what you want? What would you like to put into your collaboration, and your relationship? What do you think your co-manager would like you to contribute?

After Bridget and Howard had heard and worked on their own and each other's stories, they clearly had better impressions of each other, and the beginnings of a competitive context was replaced by a more collaborative approach. Some of the psychological energy that previously had been tied up in the victim and hero roles, the unsatisfactory situations and the desire to "pay each other back", or defend themselves against repetitions, was now released and available for collaboration. A central theme for both of them was to formulate precisely what they wanted themselves, to define their own wishes and needs, not let themselves be driven by circumstances and necessities, and not automatically take on and perform the role they imagined that the other thought they should play. It is easier to adjust to automatic reactions and patterns after getting things clear, with oneself, what sort of person one is, and what one will or will not do.

The final part of the coaching process focused on the future. The objective of the coaching was to investigate why they had ended up in this state, and whether there was any basis for continuing their collaboration. They were both able to conclude that they had understood to a large extent why things had gone the way they had, and that they felt there was a basis for continuing their collaboration. In this section, they worked on the department's strategy and priorities, the future division of the work, the level of mutual information, delegation of assignments to others, relations with the hospital management, and to how they would carry on building up their relationship and collaboration. I do not believe that Bridget and Howard came to love each other, but they did come to see each other with less interference from their own stories and patterns. They developed a respect for each other, which was characterized by each other's strengths, even though these were different from their own, and they could focus to a greater extent on their joint ambitions, which benefited the department.

Conclusion: evaluation and leave-taking

To complete their course of coaching, Bridget and Howard together evaluated the result, the process, their own work, and mine. Together, we went back over a few particular episodes and tried to understand them. In this way, there was also a chance to patch things up. Bridget felt, for example, that at the start the way she had talked about Howard's external work had been unreasonably patronizing, and she felt she ought to say so. We took our leave of each other by mentioning what had been significant for us in the process. Bridget and Howard said they were glad it was all over, because it had also been hard. They mentioned that they were nervous about whether it would all "last", but they believed it would. My evaluation, with its starting point in the role of the coach, focused on how I had experienced their work and mine, but also what working with them had meant for me personally.

The Bridget and Howard case had a "happy ending". They managed to strengthen their relationship and collaboration. It makes a considerable difference at what stage a couple come for coaching: the earlier the better. It is often the case that a couple underestimates the importance of disagreements. They see the situation as more idyllic than it is, think that the problems will go away, and that next time things will be different. It does sometimes happen that things loosen up and work out by themselves. My experience is that many couples in management—and also pairs of lovers—are under a great many external pressures in the form of expectations as to performance in their assignments and psychologically, so there is a strong likelihood of regression. Regression makes us act less like our own age in what we do. Our actions become more primitive, less accommodating and reflective, but more automatic. We develop a deficit of distance and overview about situations. Impulsive actions take over, and we get into trouble in relation to other people and to ourselves. I do not believe that coaching can be used as prophylaxis, but I think it can be a help in facing up to realities, in making allowances for the many pressures. Couples in management and lovers need to focus on their relationship now and then, and, if difficulties arise, there is no shame in asking for help.

CHAPTER FIVE

Psychodynamic coaching of groups

W e are members of groups in our everyday lives and through the course of our lives. In most cases, the family is the first meeting with a group. At one time, the family would have been defined as people who were related by blood, but this definition is no longer sufficient for the families of today. Families can be categorized as the very close family: father, mother and children, or as the slightly extended family, with the mother's and father's parents and siblings. We can go even further, to include the parents' cousins, and continue like that. A family can consist of two people, mother and child, or it can include more than two generations. Families can be large or small. Families need not be biologically related. All kinds of relationships and degrees of relationship are possible in families. Each family has its history, which, to a greater or lesser degree, defines the perception of the past and the interpretation of the present. Families can be different in all dimensions. What we have in common is that families are where most of us grow up, are formed, and form each other. The family is where we learn the fundamental things about being together with other people, for better or for worse. Anyone who has worked with people's development for many years and heard large numbers of life stories will know that all of them are unique, and that there are more "abnormal" stories than normal ones. This should start us thinking and change our ideas of what is normal in ordinary everyday conversation.

A great deal of educational and psychological research is carried on—as theory and development of practice—into families. One of the reasons for this is that the family has undergone great changes during the past century as society developed. In connection with psychodynamic coaching for groups, I will simply observe that no two families are completely identical, but they can have similarities, and it is from the family that most people gain their fundamental experiences of groups, so this will affect all the groups they belong to later, both in private life and at work. Thus, the members of any group have learnt things differently and bring many different experiences with them. There is a great deal of theory about groups, group dynamics, and group development. All this knowledge has been gathered through various ways of observing groups and their lives, by analysing "real" group situations and by constructing special events or situations for groups and then studying what happens and analysing the results of the studies. Within psychology, the discipline of social psychology is the one that has been most occupied with the study of groups.

Social psychology was originally called "mass psychology", and arose against the background of a series of observations and analyses that showed that individuals change their behaviour fundamentally when they act collectively (Olsen, 2002). A principle theory in mass psychology was that the will of the mass was the sum of the wills of the individuals, but it was later demonstrated that it was more likely that the will or character of the individual would be changed by the forces that prevailed in the group. Social psychology gradually became an independent discipline, distinct from individual psychology that centred on the single individual. Social psychology is the study of human social life. Within social psychology (Katzenelson, 1994; Mead & Morris, 1967; Sjølund, 1965) there are several different approaches to understanding groups, and correspondingly different central concepts. First and foremost, there is the distinction between a group and a mass. A group is a gathering of at least two people who have something in common. A mass is not just a large group. It is *very* large number of people—the audience at a concert, for instance—who are assembled and have a shared common feeling without this resulting in systematic collaboration. Masses are characteristically easily influenced and quick to react spontaneously.

Groups are not simply groups, either. They are divided into different categories. One way is to distinguish between primary and secondary groups. A *primary* group is a small, stable group, in which the members have strong personal links with each other—a family, for instance. In a *secondary* group the members are not so closely linked to each other, and as a rule the group is larger. It might be a group of colleagues, a school class, or those who belong to the same sports club. Groups can also be classified as formal or informal. In a *formal* group there is a goal, a fixed structure, and some rules that are intended to ensure progress towards the group's purpose. There is generally a leader or management in a formal group. Trade unions and political parties are formal groups. An *informal group* does not have the same fixed structure—a group of squatters or a supper group at a hall of residence are informal groups. There might well be leaders in informal groups, but they are not elected or appointed as leaders; as a rule, they have simply "ended up" as leaders.

In inter-group psychology (Alderfer, 1987; Jern, Boalt-Boëthuis, Hidman, & Högberg, 1984; Turner & Reynolds, 2003; Visholm, 2004) a distinction is drawn between membership groups and reference groups. People are part of a *membership group* because they have something in common with the other members. It is not necessarily a group that has any great emotional significance for anyone: it may simply be the group of non-smokers at work, or those with long hair. In contrast, a *reference group* means something special to its members, because it influences their opinions and emotions. A reference group is one that members refer to or measure up against when looking for their ideals. Thus, the reference group also influences self-perception and can be crucial to a person's actions. There is also a distinction between the *ingroup*, or own group, and the *outgroup*—"us" as opposed to "them". These designations are defined in terms of each other; the members of our own group are those who do not like the outsiders' group. Finally, there is the distinction between identity groups and purpose groups. An *identity group* is the group a person identifies with, or the group others identify him/her with, and there might, in fact, be a difference. A *purpose group* is a group with a common objective that is their reason for existence—the employees in a production company for instance.

All these designations are quite practical when a group has to be described. The groups overlap: a family group is, for instance, both a primary group and an informal group.

One of the phenomena that much of group psychology is concerned with is the concept of a *role*. Traditionally, social psychologists describe a role as the collection of expectations that a group member is expected to live up to in a particular position and situation. It might be a formal collection of expectations, set out in a job specification, for instance, or it may be informal. The informal role is not written down, but it might be orally formulated. There might also be unspoken expectations that are simply "in the air". Formal and informal roles might conflict with each other, but they can also work together. It depends entirely on the specific context. In psychodynamic system theory, the concept of a role is understood as linked to the main objective of the system—in the form of the group or organization, for instance. If the system is to achieve its objective, the main objective has to be divided into sub-objectives, and people have to perform particular actions in order to fulfil the objective. The role arises when the person meets with the system (group or organization). The psychodynamic role concept describes how the roles we are actually in can be formulated both through the conscious part of the role and its unconscious part (Krantz & Maltz, 1997; Neumann, Kellner, & Dawson, 1997; Newton, Long, & Sievers, 2006). There are roles we assume consciously, because we want to or have to. There are roles we assume because our unconscious patterns assign them to us, or because they are projected to us from other parts of the system. There are also roles that we consciously do not assume, because we do not want to or cannot, and there are roles that we unconsciously avoid, because our defences prevent it, or because our unconscious—the super-ego, for example—will not allow it. The way we fulfil our different roles is strongly influenced by our early learning and experiences in the family group. As described in Chapter Four, our experiences of siblings are extremely important here. It is in no way unusual to hear descriptions of group life referring to sibling roles. "I am so tired of always being the big sister", or "He is not taken seriously—he is just the baby or late arrival in the group".

In psychodynamic coaching for groups, the theoretical focus will obviously be on the psychodynamic understanding of what a group is, on the psychodynamic concepts of groups, on how the relational interplay between conscious and unconscious takes shape, and on the historic dimensions of the individuals' stories, the common story, and the different individuals' interpretation of the common story. Psychodynamic coaching of a group looks at the group as a whole, and at the group's internal life, and how interplay with what is outside the group affects the internal aspects in the group. The interplay *between* groups or between groups and single individuals is relevant in psychodynamic organization theory, and will be dealt with in Chapter Six.

Like the other areas of psychodynamic theory, psychodynamic group theory developed from the interaction between theory and practice, primarily in connection with clinical practice, that is, in connection with therapy. Thus, psychoanalytical group therapy has been a very influential source of development in the field. The fathers of this field are S. H. Foulkes and W. R. Bion.

Both Foulkes and Bion have inscribed themselves significantly into the psychoanalytical tradition. Both trained and practised as psychoanalysts. However, they belonged to separate psychoanalytical schools: Foulkes followed the line from Anna Freud, while Bion followed Klein's line of object relation theory, and these directions are discussed in Chapter Three in connection with the theories of personality and development. In spite of their disagreements, Foulkes and Bion do agree on certain quite fundamental aspects regarding groups: that people are basically social and that groups, therefore, are also vitally important to people, and that groups exist in their own right: they are not simply the sum of the individuals. A group is an independent unit that requires its own assumptions and concepts as the basis for psychoanalytical work. Freud himself has not written directly about groups. He did write about the "mass" or the "herd" (Freud, 1921c, 1923b). He was occupied with the processes that go on in a "mass". In the introduction to *Group Psychology and the Analysis of the Ego* (1921c), Freud admits that humans are social because "the other" is always represented in the individual's mental life.

In the mental life of the individual, the other constantly appears as a model, as an object, as an assistant and as an opponent, and thus from the start, individual psychology is also social psychology at the same time in this extended, but also entirely justifiable sense. [Freud, 1921c]

It is postulated, however (Dahlin, in Widlund, 1995), that Freud is dismissed by many later group theorists, who regard him as irrelevant in connection with studies of group dynamics, because, in the same introduction, he writes,

> However, we are likely to object that we have difficulty in assigning so much importance to the impetus given by the number that it alone should be able to call forth a new, and in other situations inactive, drive in human mental life. [Freud, 1921c]

On the surface the two statements are apparently in conflict with each other, but perhaps they indicate that Freud had thought in terms of "both . . . and". There are representatives of the other in various forms in the individual.

Being in a group, therefore, has a significant effect on single individuals, but being one of a group does not radically alter the individual's basic structure. In the clear view of posterity this does not appear as a contradiction, but simply as a description of something complex: "from the start, individual psychology is also social psychology". Moving away from individual psychology can be seen as a theoretical necessity for the development of social psychology. Things must sometimes be taken apart so that their components can be understood, and then connections and interdependencies can be studied later. Through the work of Descartes, psyche and soma were separated, leading to outstanding discoveries and knowledge of each of them separately. It would not be possible to cut people open while believing that it was the same as cutting open their souls at the same time. How, then, could a soul be sewn together afterwards? We are now living in an age when there is increasing documentation and knowledge about how psyche and soma are connected in a finely differentiated way that is not always conditional on causality. Presumably, however, we could not have come this far without the earlier separation.

Foulkes writes directly that Freud is irrelevant (Foulkes, 1984). Foulkes was more concerned with Jung as the originator of the concept of the collective unconscious and with Adler (a doctor who was a member of the close circle around Freud), who postulated that people's outer interactions form their personalities just as much as their internal drives. Discussions and arguments continue in an attempt to find the answer to the central question: what is a group? What dynamics prevail in a group? How can we understood what goes on in a group?

Both Foulkes and Bion are concerned with the interaction between the group's conscious and unconscious processes. Both are occupied with what Agazarian and Peters (1995) call the visible and the invisible group. Yet, they focus on very different parts of the group. Foulkes sees the group primarily as a healing and constructive phenomenon. Bion sees the group as a place where primitive and destructive processes occur. Foulkes and Bion were contemporaries and both worked in the 1940s at the Northfield military hospital in London. There was no formal collaboration or professional exchange between them. In his major work, *Therapeutic Group Analysis* (1984), Foulkes commented briefly on Bion's work, and on this occasion also drew attention to the differences between their analytical work. Foulkes was working on group analysis, while Bion was working with group psychotherapy. This division or distinction was maintained in the following years, and even today professional points of view are put forward supporting and maintaining the idea that the two approaches are irreconcilable. For those who are less closely associated with environments in conflict, it is easier to be less orthodox and tend more toward integration. I would assert that here, too, one can suggest that the distinction or split has given us detailed studies and knowledge about the different sides of group life, but that it is also possible to assemble these parts of the group descriptions into a more composite understanding of groups. Groups have both constructive and destructive forces and dynamics (Agazarian & Peters, 1995; Beck, 2004; Kutter, 1982).

S. H. Foulkes

Siegmund Heinrich Foulkes is the father of group analysis (Aagaard, Bechgaard, & Winther, 1994; Agazarian & Peters, 1995; Olsen, 2002; Foulkes, 1984; Heinskou & Visholm, 2004; Kutter, 1982). Foulkes was born in Germany in 1898 and fled to England, where he worked in London and then formed his first therapy group in 1940 at the Northfield military hospital. The fundamental idea of group analysis is that humans are essentially social: the individual has been formed as the result of development in the community. We are born psychologically in the social relationships that surround us, in the groups where we are members. We humans can, therefore, be understood within the social networks that we are part of. It is meaningless to try to comprehend a person isolated from them. As a consequence of this fundamental idea, people's problems, difficulties, and psychological dysfunction must also be understood as having arisen in social networks. The cure-healing—is also best when it happens in a group. The groups that have formed a person have become internalized, and are present inside that person—as a foreground or background—at all times. The aim in group analysis is the same as in psychoanalysis: to bring what is unconscious to consciousness. The treatment of the individual occurs in the process (Foulkes, 1984). The method is free discussion in the group, corresponding to free associations in psychoanalysis. Foulkes compared the individual person with a node in a neural network. There will be many different forms of communication going back and forth between the nodal points—the members: spoken and unspoken communications, conscious and unconscious communication, emotional and thought-based communication, and hypothetical communications between conceptions and fantasies. Many different kinds of communication go on in a group, at countless levels, and extending beyond the separate individuals. Foulkes took his starting point from Freud and psychoanalysis, Lewin and social psychology, Goldstein and gestalt psychology (which is different from gestalt therapy), and then from sociology, represented by Elias, which was a new science at that time.

Psychoanalysis in a group was already known. This was analysis of the individual members of the group in turn, with the other members as the therapist's "helpers". What Foulkes could see was that something happens in groups, which is *more* than in individuals, or in what could be understood as the total within the individuals. In order to pin down and grasp this phenomenon, Foulkes created the concept of the *matrix*. The matrix is a superordinate for the total of states in the group. It consists of the basic matrix and the dynamic matrix. The basic matrix refers to whatever the members of the group have in common, which is being human, often members of the same cultural society, and speaking the same language. The basic matrix concept includes what Jung called the collective unconscious. Jung was one of many sources of inspiration for Foulkes. The dynamic matrix consists of the currents in the group that are formed by all the communications arising from the differences between the members: their history, and, thus, their personalities and their current situations. The concept of the dynamic matrix—from now on called the matrix—can be compared, although it is an imperfect comparison, with a concept like "the political situation" or the concept of "traffic". We could, for instance, describe a political situation as tense, jittery, or cooling down, without it necessarily applying precisely to every individual player involved. Similarly, we could say that the traffic was aggressive this morning, without necessarily meaning that all the drivers—each and every one of them—was full of aggression. In both cases, it is a way of describing the overall state of affairs, which is more than the sum of all the individual states. The idea behind the matrix concept is that in a group there is something in addition to what the individual members contain, which is all that is between them in their relationships. Foulkes called it the "group as a whole", and it is the frame of reference for the group analysis. Group analysis is, therefore, therapy for, in, and by means of the group.

Foulkes describes this "more" that goes on through the concepts of mirroring, condensation, resonance, and context. In a group, it is possible for members to mirror themselves in each other. *Mirroring* is a collective term for the projections, identifications, and anti-identifications that go on between members. Mirroring is a benign process, which is like seeing ourselves from many sides; we may discover something new, and we are recognized and recognize others in ourselves. We are not always able to recognize ourselves in the other, if there are negative sides we wish to shake off. However, the intervention of the therapist or the other members can make a difference. *Condensation* is connected to the way that, in groups, feelings can be released because members stimulate each other to do so. If one member has spoken about performance anxiety, for instance, it is easier for others to talk about their own performance anxiety. *Resonance* means that there is a sympathetic response in the group. When one person says something, there will be different responses from different members, depending on who they are. When the various responses are shared, several possible interpretations are generated for the individual. "This could be understood differently—my way is not the only way." A special type of resonance is *polarization*, which is when something arouses opposing feelings in the group.

When something is polarized, parts that for one reason or another cannot be integrated will be split off: one can only see the good side or the bad side of something, resisting the idea that the good and the bad are linked. It could be regarded as the defence mechanism of splitting described earlier, but in this case at group level. *Context* is the social and political background that the group provides. In group analysis, this context can be investigated, understood, and developed.

In connection with psychodynamic coaching of groups, these concepts are very useful in investigating, understanding, and describing the group. What is special about this particular group? How can we understand the situation the group is in? In coaching, there is a joint project connected with whatever goal the group might have set. Foulkes postulated that there will always be many healthy forces in the group, and that the participants in the group will collectively be able to understand each other and help each other. It is striking how Foulkes was unambiguously convinced that the constructive and healing forces in the group would prevail. This may be due to the fact that the object of Foulkes's theory was a group of patients to be cured, and that the group process observed occurs with the help of one or two therapists who can propagate the healing forces. Groups in working life have no therapists. On the other hand, they have a main assignment that must be carried out. There is often a leader in a working group, but not invariably. A leader could have a therapeutic effect, understood as the ability to make the positive forces grow, but there is no guarantee. A working group, with or without a leader, might get stuck in vicious circles, becoming unproductive and undermining the members' opinion of themselves and their self-confidence. When the group is *more* than the sum of the individual parts, this can also develop in a negative direction. In his studies, Wilfred Bion developed concepts to understand these processes.

Wilfred Bion

Bion's theoretical contribution grew from work with groups of patients and groups of professionals in training (Olsen, 2002; Armstrong, 2005; Bion, 1961, 1993). Bion worked on the selection of leaders for the British army. He placed the candidates for leading positions in groups without leaders to observe what happened, who became the leader of the group and why, then what effect it had on the group, and especially on the work of the group. Bion believed that people tend to act in groups, and that this tendency originates from our childhood in the family. This group tendency is not an instinct, but one of the conditions of human life. The people who react independently of their group membership also belong to a group. Like Foulkes, Bion was interested in both the visible and the invisible group. Bion called the visible group the work group. This is a group that co-operates to achieve its task rationally and in a realistic way. Bion called the invisible group the basic assumption group. The *basic assumption group* is the state the members get into when the individuals regress because of a threat into a primitive defence position, where individuality disappears and the sense of reality is weakened.

However, the first concept Bion formulated was group culture. Group culture is the group's expression of form, that is, the group's structure and its mentality. Group mentality, in turn, is the expression of the group's will, to which the individual members contribute unconsciously. If individuals challenge the norm represented by the group mentality, they will feel uneasy, because they contribute themselves (unconsciously) to this norm. Because of the group tendency in humans, one of the things we contribute to a group is the search for security. Yet, seeking security also fills us with unease. It can be formulated as an ambivalence, where, on the one hand, we want to be part of the group, and must, therefore, fit in with this unconscious norm—the group mentality—and, on the other hand, we are afraid of disappearing—melting into the group—and losing our own distinctive character or identity. Thus, we have to balance between the urge to become part of the "group animal" and being ourselves to such an extent that we lose our membership.

When the group is in the work group state, it is reality-orientated and works towards achieving its assignment. When a threat looms up—cuts for instance—the regression pressure increases, and the group is characterized by a basic assumption state, where the members merge together more and their differences are less apparent. When the group is in the basic assumption state, it looks as if the members are working on its actual assignment, but they are not; they are working on another unconscious assignment, defined by their joint unconscious, which is a fantasy about how the group can be preserved. It looks as if they are working, but they are not, and that is why Bion calls this state an "as-if-group". Bion localized and described the three general basic assumption states, each of which has its joint fantasy.

He called one of the basic assumptions the *dependency group*. The unconscious fantasy shared by the members of the group is that if they blindly and uncritically follow their leader and the group ideas and policies, and keep the rules and regulations, they will stay together and nothing will happen. When managers complain that they get no response, ideas, or discussions with actual content from their employees at joint meetings, it might be because they are in this basic assumption state.

Another basic assumption state is characterized by the fantasy that there is a common enemy, and "if this enemy can be knocked out or we can flee from it, then we can stay together". This enemy is where all evil and all the threats are combined. The enemy might be the manager, the finance department, politicians, etc. It could even be part of the group, combined with the scapegoat phenomenon. This basic assumption group is called the *fight-and-flight group*.

The third basic assumption state described by Bion is the *pair-forming group*. The members of the group share an idealistic fantasy that something amazing is soon going to happen to the group, that something important will be created by a couple in the group. This fantasy is often about a real couple—a female member and a male member—and their creative abilities. Bion mentions that it is as if the group is waiting for "the birth of the Messiah". It can appear as if the group is waiting for the couple to make a proposal about new products that in the fantasy will save us and keep us together. What the basic assumption states have in common is that they maintain themselves, in the sense that when whatever is desired happens (we follow the leader blindly, or we conquer the enemy, or the couple makes a proposal), then it is not working as intended to gather the group together, and thus a new fantasy will arise, or the group will move towards one of the other basic assumption states.

If the group is to develop, it must move out of the basic assumption state into the working group state. Every development—even for groups—entails frustration. The group will try to defend itself against this frustration by swinging like a pendulum from idealization of the leader to devaluation and back, and expansion of the group, that is, an attempt to draw in other groups. This might be described as if the leader is afraid that a group that is functioning badly might "infect" another group. Splitting is the opposite, that is, when the group divides into subgroups. These are all everyday phenomena at workplaces.

Foulkes's and Bion's concepts provide useful implements to grasp what is going on in a group. In psychodynamic coaching for groups, it will practically always be necessary to uncover or map out *what* "in reality" is going on in the group. In the same way as with individuals and couples, it is necessary to understand why and how we ended up where we are, in order to work out a realistic strategy for the future. We know all too well when designating a scapegoat does not work, for instance, where the idea is that if only we can get rid of one of the members—the one who is slow, stupid, or strange—then we can make progress. Yet, if the one who is slow, stupid, or strange disappears, then the group will soon find a new scapegoat. This mechanism is about how the group tries to split off everything slow, stupid, or strange through projective processes, and unite in the fantasy that doing this will enable them to keep together. It is not infrequent for the scapegoat to assume the projection and identify with being slow, stupid, and different. It is an unhealthy and destructive process for everyone. If the group is to develop, then it must go through a process in which everyone takes back their projections, so that whatever is stupid, slow, or different is integrated into the group, and then adequate solutions must be found. However, it is a difficult process to go through, since it is both built up of unconscious material and emotionally frustrating.

Carl Rogers

Rogers is interesting in connection with psychodynamic coaching because of the new developments and movements he started in group psychology (Carver & Scheier, 1992; De Board, 1978; Rogers, 1971, 1992). There were two factors that stimulated his independent work. In the 1930s, he was working at a psychiatric hospital for children and adolescents in Rochester in New York, where the work of the department was based on psychoanalytical knowledge and principles. Rogers found that psychoanalysis was time-consuming and often ineffective, and he wanted to develop more effective methods. It was difficult in the hospital environment, however, because of differences of opinion between the doctors and psychologists. They disagreed about how to handle and treat specific patients, even though they agreed that what had been done was not successful. They could not agree on alternative methods of treatment either, and Rogers consequently went his own way. He moved to the group of humanistic psychologists, but never abandoned the basic psychoanalytical understandings, and in many ways maintained his own separate identity. He retained the idea of the unconscious, and of the vital importance of childhood in later life. He was especially concerned with the formation of the self, and how it influences the possibilities of living a satisfactorily life as an adult. In his opinion it is crucial to our mental health that our self-perception allows us to acknowledge the experiences we have had. The more our self-perception is congruent with our experiences and the information we receive, the better. To put it differently, referring to earlier chapters in this book, a realistic perception of oneself and the situations one brings oneself into is the best guarantee for a satisfactory life, both privately and at work.

Rogers referred to the *real self* and the *ideal self*. The closer these two are to each other, the better. There are two ways to regulate this: one is to make the self-perception more realistic, and the other is to make the ideals more realistic. Preferably, both should be done together. It is an essential point for psychodynamic coaching, the purpose of which is to set up realistic goals.

Another interesting aspect about Rogers lies in his thoughts about the role of the therapist. He proposed that the therapist should be "abolished", and that the role should be closer to an adviser and an equal. In clinical situations, I consider this problematical. In psychodynamic coaching, it is clearly stated that the totally neutral position is not possible, but that involvement with the client and the problems in hand will effectively promote development. One of the arguments in favour of the neutral position is that transferences and countertransferences then become easier to identify. In psychodynamic coaching, it is vital that involvement does not become over-involvement. It is important to register all the feelings and sensations generated by the meeting with the client or clients, since these are considered to be data in the process of coaching. Rogers made considerable use of group therapy and self-development in groups. He experimented a good deal with the role of the therapist. He found that if the open communication in the group was supported, the members would understand more and more. Instructively orientated contributions can be relevant in this connection. In the context of psychodynamic coaching, this is an obvious form of intervention on the part of the coach. An instructive definition of the concepts supports work with a hypothesis. If the members of a group are working on their mutual roles in relation to their tasks, it is a help to have a clear common definition and understanding of what a role is.

Rogers is one of a group of psychologists who formed a new tradition for working on development in groups. These development groups fall into different categories: *encounter groups,* whose purpose is to help participants to meet (encounter) the realities in their experiences more directly; *sensitivity groups* because the purpose is to increase the participants' sensitivity to their own experiences, or they are called *T-groups* (the T stands for training), where the purpose is training in how humans relate to each other. The groups developed different traditions with regard to how they were led. A characteristic of these groups was that they—unlike the groups orientated towards psychoanalysis—did not work through unstructured, free-flowing discourses, but through more structured tasks that were to be carried out and then analysed for what could be learnt from them. A very comprehensive tradition developed from these structured tasks. Annual collections were published—*The Annual Handbook for Group Facilitators* (Jones & Pfeiffer, 1979)—with exercises, describing the purpose, the actual task, and how the subsequent work on it could be organized. A task might be, for instance, that the group was to imagine that they were on a raft out at sea after an accident. They would be told what items they were allowed to have with them on the raft. The participants would have to decide—and reach agreement—on which items they would like to take with them. The group then had to discuss, share knowledge, listen, and give their reasons in order to be able to answer. If the task is to result in learning, it is vital that the participants are committed and take the task seriously. After it has been reviewed comes an analysis of the process and which roles, feelings, thoughts, and relationships came into play. There are also ideas associated with this tradition about how to work with feedback, or direct reactions between participants about the relationship, how they have perceived each other's behaviour, and what they think about it. In Denmark, a large three-volume work was published, *Strukturerede oplevelser til brug for træning i menneskelig samvirken* (Structured experiences for use in training human interaction), by Jones and Pfeiffer (1973).

The encounter tradition flourished vigorously in Denmark from the mid 1970s to the mid 1980s, but then ebbed out. This might be because there was considerable negative coverage of some of these courses in the press, where they were described as psychological assault, and professionals who take their work seriously have no wish to be associated with anything of that sort. However, the tradition has survived in various forms in management courses and training courses, although it is not particularly visible. The newer form of treatment, mentalization-based therapy (MBT), can be regarded as a development of the idea of the healing possibilities of increasing the individual's sensitivity to create a balance between experiences and self-perception. The concept of mentalization has been established in a theoretical field that integrates theories from developmental psychology, neuroscience, and psychopathology. *Mentalization* is the human ability to understand and interpret one's own and other people's intentions and actions as meaningful expressions of inner life. When we mentalize, based on our own experiences, we imagine other people's intentions based on their thoughts and feelings. Mentalization is what we do when we understand or "read" others. The way we read them is what forms the background for the way we understand ourselves. Thus, mentalization is at the heart of what, in other words, could be called emotional intelligence. The ability to reflect over what we understand in others and how we understand it, what this understanding does to us and why, is what makes fellowship with other people possible and valuable. It is also the precondition for being in the company of others in a productive way. Psychological or personal development can be understood as the development of an adaptable and reality-based capacity for mentalization (Fonagy, Gergely, Jurist, & Target, 2007). Mental illness can be understood as deviant development in the capacity for mentalization. There are obvious differences in the concepts, but it is also clear that they are related.

The idea of training the ability of the members of a group, so that they become better at reading themselves and each other, helps to make the necessary collaboration in the group more flexible. The process that the psychodynamic coaching seeks to bring about will lead to greater understanding and acceptance, and, thereby, a more accommodating approach. This was what we saw in the case of

Howard and Bridget. The structured tasks can prove valuable in psychodynamic coaching. However, they cannot carry a course of coaching alone. In a course of psychodynamic coaching with a group, it is logical for the coach to produce specific tasks for the group, orientated towards the objective of the coaching. Group tasks and individual but identical tasks for the participants in the group will structure the quantity of data and make it easier to overcome the work of dealing with something as complex as a group.

The starting point for psychodynamic coaching in groups will be the psychodynamic theories and concepts about groups. The aim is that the group must connect its past (i.e., the individual histories, the group's common history and relationships) to the present and the current situation, in order to create an understanding and acknowledgement that can form the framework for a realistic future. As in psychodynamic coaching for couples, the group might in the end remain together, or it is possible that the group or parts of the group will split up. The coach will be aware that each participant has a personal history, and that the group can bring out different valencies in the individual. In groups there might also be collusions, for instance, between the leader and the members, or between parts of the membership. When Foulkes recommends that the therapist should make use of freely floating attention to be able to grasp the character of the matrix, this also applies to the task of coaching. A group is an enormously complex unit, and there are many individual parts to be picked up, and many transferences and countertransferences. In psychodynamic coaching, the focus is on the goal. In the work of coaching a group, it is critical to have a clear definition of the goal and a carefully prepared description of the current state of affairs if focus is to be maintained on what is relevant, so that one is not distracted by all the other currents and interests in the group. If one of the objectives specifically is to increase the empathy of the group members for each other, then here-and-now sessions are appropriate. They can be linked to the group's there-and-then, thus forming the link between past and present. The following is a description of a course of coaching with a group.

Case: the designer team

This case description is structured like the other descriptions, as the course of psychodynamic coaching is to be organized.

The client's first contact

The HR director of a clothing manufacturing company contacted me by e-mail. She had a high-performance designer team that had got itself into conflicts. Would it be possible for me to take on the task? If so, how long would I estimate it would take? Could I give her an idea of the economics involved? The e-mail signalled a certain "consumer consciousness". "I-know-what-I-want-so-can-you-deliver-it?" Speed, efficiency, and, without it being mentioned explicitly, I sensed that I should probably answer or react rapidly, which I did.

I sent an e-mail, which suited me well, because then I could be similarly precise and direct, and communicate exactly what I wanted to say. I replied that I could certainly take on the task, if they could wait until there was space in the calendar (and I indicated when that would be), but that I needed to know more about the assignment before I could begin to calculate time and money. It was a very long time before I heard from the HR director again. I had almost forgotten them, when an e-mail turned up with the answer that they could manage it. They suggested that I should book an appointment for the first meeting with the group, and on the basis of that, agree on the framework for the course. It seemed straightforward and just a little too easy. The appointments fell into place, and we were still carrying on all communications by e-mail. I made no effort to ring. I found some details about the company on the Internet, but avoided direct contact.

The first coaching session: objectives and framework

The group consisted of five members: Louise, Kasper, Aja, Sanne, and Patrick. They were all aged about thirty, and looked very cool and organized. I had arranged a circle of chairs for us to sit on—there were no tables. I welcomed them, introduced myself, and explained the background of the appointment and what the task for that session would be: to decide on the objective of our work and agree on how many times and how often we would meet. I asked them to introduce themselves. After the round of introductions, I asked them to explain why they had come. I had deliberately not asked them individually or asked them to take turns. I addressed them as a group. Patrick spoke up. Patrick was from England and spoke Danish with a slight, but charming accent. He explained that they were the team that designed children's clothes. In the previous season, their clothes had sold really badly. They had launched a new concept consisting of four different types of clothes, intended to suit four different types of children: the Country Girl, the Daredevil, the Princess, and the Gallant Knight. Their plan had been to follow up on the idea, but since sales were so far from satisfactory, they were asked to find something different. They were really furious with the management. The designer team believed that the reason for the poor sales figures was that the marketing department had not supported the idea properly with a campaign that matched the concept. No one would listen to that round of criticism, and the management insisted on the demand for new thinking. Internally, the group had discussed the development process and who had been responsible for what. Sanne, who had been in charge of contact with the marketing department, had felt she was being mobbed, and was extremely uncomfortable with the rest of the group. At an employee development interview she had broken down, burst into tears and said she was under stress because of the psychological working environment in the team. So, the HR department had been asked to work with the team. An assessment of the workplace was carried out, which showed that no one in the group was really happy about it. One of the HR staff had a meeting with the team, and observed that it was not within her capabilities to take on the task, so this was why I had been contacted. All this was common knowledge. Patrick told the story without interruption from the others.

After this account, I asked them—still addressing the whole group—how they would define the difficulties in their situation. Aja was the first to answer: "We need to let bygones be bygones and look ahead. I think we should focus more on what is going well, and forget about the rest—that is what business is like—and we should just move on, without getting so sentimental." "It is so not-cool to keep tramping about in all this," said Louise. Sanne said, "I want to be one of the group again, but I feel the reproach hanging over my head all the time, and it hampers my creativity." Kasper said nothing. There was silence. It lasted so long that it became uncomfortable, and Patrick said, "This is crazy! It's more like us to be all talking at once!" I pointed out that it would be more helpful here at the beginning if they could say more about what they thought was difficult, and less about what they thought should be done. Things went very slowly. Kasper had not said anything at all. When time ran out, we had not come much closer to a definition of the central problems or a goal for the coaching. I observed that it would only be possible to work together and make progress if they decided to co-operate, talking openly, with open ears and open minds. I said, "I can't just conjure up a solution, much as I would like to. If you are going to develop, you must be prepared for a demanding, but also a very interesting piece of work."

I think it was too difficult for them, because I addressed them as an entity, as a group. My hypothesis was that they felt like single individuals who were unfortunately forced to work together, so when I talked to them as a group, everything tightened up inside them: as they understood things, they were original, separate individuals, or artists who should not be lumped together in a group. They were afraid of being swallowed up by the group "animal" and losing their personal characteristics. Therefore, I changed my strategy—without sharing this hypothesis with them—and set them an exercise in the next session. They all had to answer the following questions in writing: What do you most want to change in this team? How did you feel when you first joined the team? How do you feel about it now? What essential characteristics do you have in common with other members of the team? What essential differences are there between you and the other team members? Do you want to work in this team? Why? Or why not? Do you believe in a joint future for the team? They seemed overwhelmed by this exercise, but they accepted it.

In the next session, I carried on working with the hypothesis from the previous session: if there was any truth in it, then a way into the group would be to make sure that they each felt they were being considered with their distinctive characteristics, so that they could be more present and get involved, and work out whether there was any basis for a course of coaching. I controlled the proceedings more than in the first session. I asked them to answer in turn. One question at a time. It became obvious that nobody felt there were any similarities, and, by contrast, there were lots of differences. They wanted to change very different aspects, but most of the changes involved smaller teams and more individual work. Some did not want to work in the team at all, while others could see that some assignments were best carried out in a team. I took great care to write things on a flip-chart, so that they could all see that their answers were being taken seriously. When the round of answers was over, I repeated the aim of the coaching. I wanted to ask them to look carefully at everything that was written on the flip-chart, and consider freely what the goal for the coaching might be, *if* there was going to be any coaching. It was as if it was dawning on them for the first time that the coaching did not *necessarily* have to end with them staying together, and that they did not necessarily have to agree to coaching. My hypothesis was that since they had been seen by me as individuals, and they had been allowed to show themselves to the others as individuals, they would be able to listen. This was when they realized for the first time that they had the freedom to take part in a joint decision.

The story was told about another team who had got into conflicts, and they had their fantasies that I had been given secret instructions by the management to find out which of them were to be dismissed! It took yet another session before the goal was in place. It was decided that the goal would be to find out why they were so afraid (I would call it paranoid) about being in the group, and they should find out which areas it would be sensible to work in separately, and in which areas it would be an advantage for them to work as a team. The time schedule was settled as six whole days from 9 a.m. to 4 p.m, two days in each of the first two months, and then one day in each of the following two months. With groups, it is an advantage to have a longer periods of time. There are more of them, and there is more to be said and listened to. There is a risk that things become too fragmented if the sessions are divided up too much, and altogether it can take longer.

The course of coaching

The days were all structured in the same way: four working sessions with different tasks and breaks at intervals between them (see Appendix 5). The group went through the personal histories told by all the members, and, especially, the stories of siblings led to acknowledgements. The process and its content made it possible to work with relationships and feelings. They managed to investigate what they had in common, the group, how the group affected them, and what importance the common history had. They mentioned the intense rivalry in the group to be the greatest and most talented artist, and it became obvious in what way the surrounding organization contributed to this rivalry through secret salaries and extra rewards, promotions, or trips to the East to visit suppliers and factories. Their ambitions were brought into the open, and their dependency on their jobs became clear.

Their valencies for playing particular roles were mapped out. Two members of the group had once been lovers, and they had decided that this meant nothing—once it was over, then it was over. But it had not turned out like that, and the wounded partner had found a lot of sly ways to take revenge: for example, "accidentally" changing the colour code in a proposal. A lot of admissions came to light along the way. The healing forces were stimulated by the mirroring and resonance that arose during the process. They found it difficult to relate to the future. Having to secure their own success seemed an insurmountable obstacle. The pressure sent them repeatedly back to basic assumption states. They alternated most between dependency and fight-or-flight. After a brief description of the concepts (a sort of miniature teaching session), they became increasingly aware of when it happened, or rather, when it had happened, because it was most usual that they discovered it afterwards, either alone or when reflecting together. They had started to hold "process meetings" about their co-operation once a week. In the coaching sessions with the theme exercise, it became possible to work with the system perspective.

The team had been "caught" in an unconscious inter-group dynamic with the marketing department. The team's defence had been to deny that the internal rivalry had been one of the causes of their sales fiasco: the product was simply not good enough, because they had not worked on it sufficiently openly and thoroughly. They had kept back ideas, for example, that might have improved parts of the others' contributions, because they did not want them to succeed. They had stifled each other's good ideas in envy of the others' creativity. They had put obstacles in the way of each other's sources of inspiration, and, at times, prototypes had been inexplicably delayed. In the denial of these very fatiguing internal relationships, they had unconsciously reached agreement that the "villain" was the marketing department, without reality-testing this explanation by having a meeting with anyone from the marketing department. The team had "sent" Sanne as the representative to the marketing department; she was the team member who was most "different", more conventional and less ambitious. When Sanne did not succeed in getting the marketing department to co-operate, it confirmed the team's projective fantasy that everything that flopped was linked to Sanne, so, if it was not the marketing department, then it must be Sanne who was the reason for the lack of success. Sanne had taken this projection to herself, and was weighed down by it.

The projective identification process was broken down during the coaching as the other members of the group withdrew their projections through detailed discussions, especially of the creative part of the design process. In turn, it confirmed for the marketing department how weak people were in the design team by identifying the entire team with Sanne, its representative. In this way the two groups—the team and the marketing department—got into a mutual projective relationship that prevented actual collaboration. The team were angry with the management for not stepping in. This can be understood as another form of defence: the basic assumption of dependency. On their part, the management had not stepped in because its members did not agree among themselves about the structure the company should have. At a conference day for employees, some of them had spoken in favour of a matrix-inspired organization, in which product development would go on in groups consisting of employees from different departments. Others were in favour of returning to separate creative workshops for designers with the other departments as support departments. The management could not agree among themselves. This lack of clarity and the anxiety it had generated had reinforced the unproductive basic assumption states, most clearly as fight-or-flight, but also as dependency. The marketing department and the designer team had unconsciously ended up acting out the management disagreements. The unconscious assignment they had been set was to test the value of the present organization.

As the team acknowledged having been part of these collective projective processes, it "woke them up", and made them want to test the reality of the many accepted "truths". They fixed times and held meetings with the marketing department, so that they could investigate their fantasies about the connection between the low sales and the campaign. They had a meeting with the management, to ask what future plans they had for the team. They made plans for the next season, but could not manage to go further. They could not see over to the other side of the success or fiasco measurement. One of the members wanted to travel the world and take up challenges in other places.

Conclusion: evaluation and leave-taking

When a course has been organized over whole days, things happen in the attachment between the coach and the client group. As a consequence of the intensity and the duration, the task and the relationships are very prominent.

The group managed jointly to evaluate the process, the result, their work, and mine. Together, we went back over a few particular episodes and tried to understand them. They were especially surprised at how "cheese-paring" they had been about talking at the beginning. "What did you do to get us to start talking?" they asked. I shared my early hypothesis with them. Someone shouted spontaneously, "Cheating!" They laughed a lot about that. On the one hand, there was relief that they had been "discovered" so early on, and, on the other hand, irritation over someone else seeing something in them that they could not see themselves. Aja, who was a little more impulsive than the others, wanted, as she put it, to take back some of the things she had said. At the end of this course, too, they each took their leave by mentioning what they had found especially significant in the process. The important thing about rounding off a course properly and attentively is that it is a way of showing how the relationship has been valued, and it is good training in saying goodbye and, thus, going out of the relationship with empathy. When the ending gathers up the whole, it strengthens what has been learnt, and, thereby, the progress that is made.

CHAPTER SIX

Psychodynamic coaching in organizations

P sychodynamic organizational psychology is a branch of the discipline of organizational psychology. At the same time, psychodynamic organizational psychology also includes elements from many psychodynamic branches of other disciplines in psychology, and these are the psychology of personality, developmental psychology, couple psychology, group psychology, social psychology, and parts of psychopathology. Figure 1 in Chapter One is an attempt to illustrate this, and is also the basis for the structure of this book. This arrangement gives an idea of fractal interrelationships, where the whole is found in the parts and the parts in the whole. Perhaps that is one of the reasons why it is so fascinating to work with psychodynamic organizational psychology. It is extensive, widely embracing, and multi-faceted, as opposed to fragmented and selective. This does not mean it is less deep, however. One could say, on the contrary. There are many specific and in-depth contributions in psychodynamic organizational psychology. When one has to grasp a particular phenomenon in organizational psychology, and is faced in practice with a problem in organizational psychology, the psychodynamic approach is highly suitable. The theory and concepts in themselves carry the inspiration for organizational psychological designs.

In my experience, the psychodynamic approach is effective in the sense that with these interpretations at the back of one's mind, it is possible to create solutions in organizations that can, in fact, promote mental health and sound growth. These solutions can be liberating and release tension, bringing qualitative development in both individuals and systems. The process might be difficult and frustrating, and will call for hard work, because it *is* difficult to develop oneself, abandoning long-held attitudes and points of view, or relinquishing well-known feelings, accepted facts, and familiar patterns. It *can* be difficult and painful to have to work at reassessing significant relationships and self-images, because reality does not always fit into our ideal wishes, but causes anxiety instead. Psychodynamic understanding can grasp the complexity and generate lasting solutions. Creating short-term success, euphoria, and enthusiasm does not require in-depth knowledge, only an ability to "sell ideas" and beguile others.

Psychodynamic system theory

Psychodynamic organizational psychology and the psychodynamic system theory centrally embedded in it are well described in other works. All the central concepts and areas of application are mentioned in Heinskou and Visholm (2004). Only the absolute core concepts will be explained here.

Von Bertalanffy (1968) formulated the open system theory, which springs from the living systems of biology. A cell has a *primary task*, as a rule to grow, so that it can divide itself. If this is to succeed, the cell must balance in a relationship of exchanges with its surroundings. Elements and resources must be brought in from outside, which enter the cell through the cell wall, the limits of the cell system. Inside the cell, they are processed, and the cell absorbs nourishment from the incoming resources. As a side effect, the process will generate waste substances that must be passed out of the system through the cell wall. The cell's primary task justifies its existence. The precondition for carrying out the task is that the cell is in an exchange relationship with its surroundings, that the cell wall is permeable, and that the internal parts of the cell can identify what should be allowed to enter or be drawn in. Miller and Rice stated in 1975 that the same principles apply to social systems populated by humans. Social systems, whether families or organizations, follow the same basic principle. Here, too, the primary task and limits are central concepts. An efficiently running and healthy social system has a clear primary task and limits that allow resources and waste to be passed in and out. If the limits are not open enough, life in the system will come to a standstill, and if they are too open, there will be difficulty in sorting the exchanges, which can cause difficulty in carrying out the primary task, because the incoming and outgoing streams of resources will be uncontrolled.

If the social system is a family, for instance, and the limits are too narrow, so that the family does not have contact and interaction with the world around it, this will lead to unhealthy developments, hindering the family from completing the primary task, which is to ensure development tasks for all the members corresponding to their age. The children in the family should gradually learn to manage without their parents, so they are eventually ready to leave the nest. When the family limits are too confined, abuse and ill treatment occur. The surrounding society cannot "see into" the family system, and cannot see what is happening, while the members cannot "see" out, make contacts, and tell others about the abuse or make it visible. The limits might be too open, as in some modern families consisting of active, busy, and career-minded parents with children of different marriages—"his, hers, and joint" children. All the members of the family have many activities outside the home, and lots of friends who come and go, while some of the children sometimes live with this family and sometimes with their other parent. In some families, there might be uncertainty about who the members of the system are and when, who is at home and when, or who is in charge of what, and who is responsible for seeing that the developments at each age are actually started and completed. In families like that, no one might discover that the primary task is not being performed before the parents suffer from stress or depression, and the grown-up children will not move away, prefer eating Coco-pops with milk for breakfast, lunch, and tea, and do not know how to set the washing machine to do a hot-wash cycle. The concepts of a primary task and limits are equally useful in identifying the problems in a system like that, whether it is too closed or too open.

Miller and Rice (1975) add that the objective of the system is to survive, and that a healthy system will endeavour to find and maintain the right "permeability" in the limits, which is a management task. Since it is a system consisting of people, the forces and dynamics that people and relationships bring with them and are subject to will also prevail in the system. The open system theory is, thereby, extended to become the psychodynamic system theory. It means that the system must also be understood on the basis of the prevailing psychodynamics. There will be rational and irrational processes in a system. The rational processes are conscious processes directed towards carrying out the primary task, while the irrational processes are everything that goes on at the same time. The irrational processes are unconscious processes that give rise to activities that are not directed towards the primary task, but towards the unconscious motives. In a system, conscious and unconscious roles will arise, as described in earlier chapters. The rational and irrational processes and activities enter into a complex interaction. This interaction might be beneficial and support the performance of the primary task, or the opposite might be the case. If the external pressure becomes too great, a system will regress, just as people do. The external pressure might come from increased competition, technological developments, fewer resources, or processes of change such as mergers and demergers.

Regression in systems might lead to the emergence of scapegoats and basic assumption states (see Chapter Five) in part-systems or groups. *The management's* responsibility is to ensure that the primary task is carried out. To do this, they must be "border guards", that is, they must make sure that the border has the optimum degree of permeability for carrying out the primary task. With the exchanges between the system and its surroundings suitably managed and controlled, it will not fall behind in product development, for instance, or start up more product development projects than resources will allow, while employees receive supplementary training, but are not away on courses all the time, which would prevent them from producing enough, etc. For management to be successful, it must have a certain authority. *Authority* (Jaques, 1976; Obholzer, 1994; Visholm, 2004) comes from above, below, and within. From higher up in the system means from the Board or from the members, who, through a democratic process, have delegated the authority. Authority from below comes from those who are to be managed, meaning that they accept management because, in their eyes, the leaders have qualified themselves. From within means from oneself, from having a personality that can fill oneself with a feeling of authority.

Within the system, there are generally a number of different part-systems, each of which can be considered as a sub-system and described and analysed using the same concepts as the "large" system. Another important aspect of understanding systems is the activity—rational and irrational—that goes on between groups and in groups, seen from the perspective of the relationships they have with other groups. Inter-group psychology has its roots in social psychology. In inter-group psychology, all the members of the group are understood as the single individuals they are, but, at the same time, each is a representative of the whole group (Alderfer, 1987; Heinskou & Visholm, 2004). If one of the teachers at a school is permissive and lazy, the parents might, for example, see him as representative of *all* the teachers at the school. Similarly, if one employee from the auditing section in a company is very dominating and over-zealous about his work, the members of other departments might regard all auditors in the finance department as equally over-zealous and dominating. In organizations there will be countless examples of such generalizations, which in practice rarely stand up to a reality test: as a rule, the members of a group are more differentiated from each other.

However, groups can, consciously or unconsciously, make use of a single member as a representative, someone who must do things on behalf of the group. A welfare officer from the local authority's social services department contacts a colleague from the children's and youth section to collaborate about a family. The team in the social services department has unconsciously chosen a person who is somewhat inflexible as a representative, because they are not really interested in collaboration, since in their view it will be extremely time-consuming. He is also rejected by the children's and youth section, and this episode leads the social services department to form opinions about whether it is at all possible to set up collaboration across the departments. Thus, the dynamics between groups is linked to group dynamics, the personalities of the individual group members, and the internal relationships between the members. This is an important perspective to be aware of in psychodynamic coaching: what inter-group dynamics are active in the system the client comes from? Is the client "serving" or being regarded as the representative of his/her group?

As mentioned at the beginning of the book, the system is always present in psychodynamic coaching. It is important to be able to maintain the system perspective in a course of coaching to be able to understand the dynamics of the system, which are co-players in the client's situation, and to see the client's actions, thoughts, and feelings also as products of the projective processes in the system. A feeling of inadequacy or incompetence can be understood as a projective identification process. It is important to keep the system perspective open, both in "private" or self-initiated psychodynamic coaching and in coaching that goes on in organizations, in precisely the same way as it is important to maintain the personal and individual perspective. This is what makes psychodynamic coaching exciting, demanding, and effective.

When is coaching appropriate in organizations?

Among the many approaches to coaching that are not based on theory or concepts, the coaching style of management is often referred to using expressions such as "the manager as coach". From a psychodynamic perspective, this lacks a rational foundation. Between managers and employees there is a relationship of authority, or, in other words, power is applied. This is incompatible with the basic principle of psychodynamic coaching (as it should be with all coaching) for two reasons.

The first—as illustrated in the foregoing chapters—is that the issues on which coaching works are extremely personal, perhaps sensitive, private circumstances. This is irreconcilable with a relationship of authority. In Denmark, where practically everyone with a short or medium-length training in the field of Humanities has read Habermas (1981) and knows the concept of the "dominance-free discourse", it is surprising that anyone has succeeded in introducing the phenomenon. Habermas describes when a discourse is "valid and binding" in an ethical sense. It will be when the participants are speaking sincerely and in accordance with what they believe to be true, and when reasoning is what counts, when there is no domination from subjective interests or relations of authority, and when the discourse refers solely to general norms for all affected by the discourse. What Habermas demands is an ideal that can probably never be achieved in reality, but it fulfils the function of an ideal from an ethical point of view as the objective to strive for. A course of coaching between two people where one has system-based authority over the other is not an attractive proposition. It cannot seem a relevant idea in any way when psychodynamic knowledge of unconscious motives is coupled with the challenge of Habermas. When coaching is dealing with the personal development of the less powerful of the two parties, the manager acting as coach is completely unacceptable. If we are to find justification for the fact that, nevertheless, one meets the idea of the manager as coach, it must be attributed to incentives other than stimulating development in the employee. It might be due to ignorance, inability to see the implications, or lack of insight. It might be the seduction of consultant firms and their promises to enhance the management's competence and efficiency, or avoid inconvenience— with underlying economic interests—as strong motivation. There might also be speculative ideas of coaching as socialization, encouraging conformity and assimilation, where force is disguised as development and learning.

A second reason why the "Manager as coach" is not an appropriate idea is that a manager will very rarely be suitably trained to play the role of the coach. This applies in any case to psychodynamic coaching. There are comments on other approaches to coaching in Chapter One, but obviously, in these more or less theoryless approaches, one will find claims that a course lasting three or four weeks should qualify a manager to act as a coach for his/her employees. Thus, the psychodynamic understanding of coaching does not consider it possible between members of an organization. Even if it is done by an internal HR employee, it is problematical, because he or she is a member of the same system as the person who is to be coached. Internal HR functions are sometimes asked to plan and conduct processes that very closely resemble actions to promote occupational satisfaction, but are, in fact, strategic socialization in the interest of the organization.

Psychodynamic coaching is relevant in other situations in an organization. These might be in connection with management courses, conflict solving and problems in collaboration, prophylactic measures in processes of change, and as an offer to employees with specific difficulties. Still, some preconditions must be met with reference to the reasons above, if it is to be ethical and professionally justifiable. When it is the organization that instigates the coaching, it is quite crucial that a free relationship is established between the coach and the clients. In other words, there must not be any other relationships between the client and coach beside the fact that one is a coach for the other. Another precondition is that the coach is trained for psychodynamic coaching (see Chapter Three). If the coaching is part of a management training programme or a management course, then coaching can be carried out in the same place. In other cases coaching should preferably take place in a neutral setting, such as the coach's work premises, but not in the coach's own home. The reason for this is that the setting will then support the freedom of the relationship. If the coaching takes place in the company premises, it feeds fantasies of relationships between the company owners or the senior management and the coach. Even if the coaching does take place in a neutral setting, this is no guarantee against hidden motives, as was seen in the case of the designer team. If the coaching takes place on organization premises, this will almost provide support for paranoid—but not abnormal—fantasies. In any case, it is important that any such fantasies can be dealt with. The coach's own home is unsuitable for coaching because it makes it impossible to act "personally but committed to the role". The personal side will take over, because there is so much that is personal and private in most homes, which will make it difficult to maintain the role.

Management courses and coaching

The example of John in Chapter One was taken from coaching arranged in connection with a management course. This management course consisted of a number of different elements: presentations on leadership and organizational psychology, group exercises, group dynamic exercises, etc. In between the various elements, the programme included individual psychodynamic coaching and coaching in groups. The individual coaching worked in accordance with the idea in psychodynamic coaching, but here with the number of sessions agreed on in advance. The coaching in the course group was "in" and "by" the group. The group itself was not being coached as in Chapter Five. The reason for this was that the group only existed as a group in the context of the course, which naturally did not eliminate the group dynamics at play in the "group as a whole", but, because of the time aspect, this angle was played down in this connection. "In" the group means that participants individually, in the hearing of the others, presented a side of their role as manager that they wanted to work on, and a target for it that they would like to achieve by working on it in the course group. The coach led the work, and the task of the group was to function as a reflective and associated sounding board and mirror. The same coach worked with the group and in the individual sessions. This made it possible to bring data from the group coaching sessions to the individual coaching, but never in the opposite direction. Both areas are covered by confidentiality and the duty of professional secrecy, but common experiences can always be included.

Another way to structure coaching in connection with management training is to keep it separate from the seminars and the residential course, and instead run it as parallel or individual coaching, or group coaching. It is not entirely comparable with the "ordinary" individual coaching courses, where people seek coaching independently of the company they work for. In cases where coaching is part of the management training, it will obviously make a difference that the organization has decided on the framework and it is the organization that pays. The client's responsibility for achieving the goal within the framework may be affected by this. If possible, it is best if the coach is not a member of the team that is arranging the earlier part of the management training. It supports the freedom in the relationship and, thus, the work of coaching. One might find that companies want to decide which themes are to be dealt with during coaching. This must be refused. Binding of any kind is irreconcilable with the entire foundation of psychodynamic coaching and its ethics.

Psychodynamic coaching as an offer to managers and employees who are in difficulties

As part of a kind of "welfare policy", some organizations offer to pay for psychodynamic coaching for their employees. It might be in connection with situations at the workplace, or it might be in connection with private problems. Considered from a psychodynamic point of view, the two areas are linked, but personal valencies and patterns can be, or become, difficult in one context but not in another. Clients whose coaching is paid for by their workplace are "treated" in every sense like all other clients. However, the fact that they do not pay for it themselves creates a dependency that might affect and influence the work. There may be pressure to achieve something: "I must develop in a direction that is satisfactory for the company, and as fast as possible". It could lead to concern that someone in the organization might ask how things are going, either out of friendly interest, or, for example, in connection with an employee development interview. It might get entangled in financial dependency: "I am in the middle of a development process, and have heard that I must change my job—but if I do, my coaching will not be paid for, and my development will be interrupted". This is why it is important, if the company pays, to mention these factors and be aware of their psychodynamic significance.

A coach who works with several clients from the same company will, as a rule, receive plenty of data about the same phenomena. In cases like these, the coach's professional capacity for working with boundaries, keeping issues separated, and with self-reflection is important. It is also necessary to reflect over one's own dependencies and tendencies when agreements are to be worked out with companies. It means that it is a central principle to keep to the straight and narrow path and not be tempted to make agreements that hinder the uninhibited work relation between coach and client. Written formulations—although they cannot provide a complete guarantee—are preferable, so that no unfortunate situations arise through misunderstandings about goals, means, and time, etc.

Solving conflicts and collaboration problems

Psychodynamic coaching is not the solution to everything. There are many well-founded ways of working on solving conflicts and collaboration problems in organizations that have nothing to do with coaching. These methods and concepts are anchored in psychodynamic organization psychology. Coaching is not in any way a relevant replacement for them. Psychodynamic coaching is relevant in connection with conflicts and difficulties in co-operation in organizations when they are related to internal conflicts in management groups or in a couple in management. The work will then proceed as in the cases described earlier with reference to couples and groups. Still, in some cases, there might be an advantage in the fact that at the same time, between the client and the coach and as an element of the work, an analysis is done of the organizational state. There will be moments when the coach's role will be more that of a guide than a coach, as it will also draw on the coach's specialist knowledge of organizational dynamics. One of the elements that, for instance, can be handled during a working day with a management group struggling with conflict could be an analysis of the organization, examining the significance of the state of the organization in relation to the management group as individuals and as a group. It is beyond the scope of this book to describe how such analyses can be carried out, but there is literature from both theoretical and practical approaches to this area. Naturally, managers who have become entangled in conflicts can also ask for coaching, but they must be considered as individual courses of coaching, with the same reservations as described above if they are paid for by the organization.

Prophylactic measures in connection with processes of change

The last form of psychodynamic coaching in organizations that will be described here is when it is included as part of a process of change in an organization. Some executive boards and managements appreciate that going through change can be psychologically demanding for employees, both at management and operator level.

Processes of change cause anxiety and also bring losses at different levels, resulting in grieving to a greater or lesser degree (Heinskou & Visholm, 2004; Hirschhorn, 1995, 2000; Jaques, 1971; Menzies, 1975). To support the process of change, some executive boards provide opportunities for managers to be coached. Their motives might be partly humanitarian, showing that they want to take good care of important colleagues, and partly strategic, since it facilitates the process of change if space is allowed for working out both anxiety and grief, so that it paves the way for a positive and co-operative approach instead of resistance. This raises the question of whether it is at all possible for coaching to have a prophylactic purpose. If the idea is that being coached will reinforce general robustness as a kind of insurance policy, then the answer is no, it will not work. That would be like putting a leg in plaster (to have it ready in advance) in case you broke your leg, or taking pain-killers in the morning to prevent a headache later in the day. If the aim is to strengthen oneself generally to face the challenges of life, then it is better to have psychotherapy, which is like strengthening one's body through a healthy lifestyle. If there is to be any meaning in the idea of prophylactic coaching, the offer must be made after the change is announced, when the anxiety wells up, and the natural thought reaction is "how will it affect me?" The coaching must follow the same principles as described earlier, and there must be a personal goal or a group goal. In a changing situation, other forms of organizational psychological consultation might also be appropriate, or perhaps even more so.

Precisely because there has been—and still is—so much uncertainty about what coaching is (and is not), there has been a tendency to regard coaching as the answer to all tribulations. The psychodynamic tradition in organizational psychology has developed many methods that can be used in targeted consultation. Whether the answer in connection with a specific request from a company is coaching or another form of consultation must depend on what the main purpose of the intervention is. Psychodynamic coaching is one method founded on theory, not a universal cure. It is important for a coach to be critical and self-reflective in deciding whether to make use of one method or another. It is naturally easier for the consultant if she can also offer other psychodynamic methods, and not only coaching.

CHAPTER SEVEN

Psychodynamic practice

T he psychodynamic coaching described here has drawn its inspiration from other psychodynamic methods. Psychodynamic coaching is not a modern designation for psychotherapy, or the same as role analysis or supervision. Psychodynamic coaching is an independent method in its own right, drawing its theoretical base from the same fields of knowledge as the other psychodynamic methods. I would like to clarify and delimit psychodynamic coaching from other methods, and in this chapter I briefly describe psychodynamic coaching in comparison with other psychodynamic methods, to make the differences and similarities clear. The intention is to make it clear for those who want to make use of psychodynamic coaching where the borderlines are with other methods.

Psychoanalysis as a method

Psychoanalysis is the overall name for the extensive field of psychoanalytical theory that originated in Freud's theory of drives, theory of personality, and development theory. Psychoanalysis is also the name of a method. The objective of psychoanalysis is to bring the unconscious to consciousness, so that inner tensions can be relieved or reorganized. Psychoanalysis has its origins in hypnotism. When the patient is under the influence of hypnosis, the psychoanalyst can gain insights into the patient's unconscious, since hypnosis effectively opens the way. However, the difficulty with hypnosis proved to be that when the patient came out of hypnosis, there were no permanent changes in the inner states of tension. The original situation was recreated. Freud "invented" another method by which the unconscious could be "opened" while the patient was fully conscious. This technique consisted of an exchange of words between the patient and the analyst. Speech is the psychoanalyst's most important tool. The patient does most of the talking, according to the principle of free associations and ideas. The analyst listens attentively and contributes interpretations. The setting for psychoanalysis is that the patient lies on a couch, with the analyst sitting in a chair a short distance from the patient's headrest, beyond the view of the patient, because the patient must not be distracted by observing the analyst's facial expressions or the like. The rule for what the patient says is that he or she must say whatever comes to mind, and express the associations that follow on.

If the therapy is to succeed, the rule of abstinence must be observed. This *rule of abstinence* is the principle of the analyst's complete neutrality. It means that social rules that apply in other forms of conversation are suspended in the psychoanalytical room. The analyst does not answer questions, and does not react to expressions of emotion or attitude from the patient. The analyst listens and brings "freely floating attention" into play. This "freely floating attention" is an expression of the state the analyst assumes in order to listen fastidiously at several levels all at once. There must not be any other relationship between the patient and the analyst apart from the relationship in the therapy room. The analyst must not in any way follow his or her own impulses to react to countertransferences. Observation of the rule of abstinence protects the analyst against his or her own affectations and provides the patient with the best guarantee that the therapy will be effective. It is observation of the rule of abstinence that makes a cure possible. This rule of abstinence is also called the gold standard of psychoanalysis. Originally, psychoanalysis was designed and intended for patients suffering from psychological dysfunction. It is now also sought by people who want therapy in order to improve their quality of life. Psychoanalysts must have been psychoanalysed themselves before they may practise, so a number of psychoanalysts are also occupied in analysing future analysts.

Psychodynamic coaching differs from psychoanalysis in the part of the objective that concerns healing. Psychodynamic coaching is not for people suffering from mental disorders of a pathological nature. However, psychodynamic coaching resembles psychoanalysis with regard to opening and uncovering the client's unconscious and preconscious areas. Psychoanalytical coaching also works with countertransference, but in a different way from psychoanalysis. There is the same understanding of the concepts of transference and countertransference. The rule of abstinence is also present in a modified form. In the previous chapters, it has been referred to in connection with psychodynamic coaching as the free relationship. There must be no relationship between the client and the coach other than the actual relationship of client and coach, and the coach must not react on impulse or normatively in relation to the client.

In psychodynamic coaching, the coach plays an active part, openly drawing in countertransferences, interpretations, and hypotheses as data on what is going on within the client, and what is going on in the relationship between the client and the coach. It is called "personal engagement in the role". This is possible on the precondition that the coach is reflective and self-reflective, with a general stability with regard to impulses and emotions. It is, therefore, a requirement that the coach must be trained in a way that includes therapy and/or analysis. The client is involved in the work of interpretation in the course of working on the problem and working through to the goal. Psychodynamic coaching also diverges from psychoanalysis in another critical direction, in that a goal is defined for the process, which then determines what is understood as relevant or irrelevant. Psychoanalysis is a very time-consuming method of treatment, and a patient will often attend sessions two or three times a week for several years. Psychodynamic coaching takes place over a shorter period, with a pre-arranged time limit (Bering, 1989; Freud, 1933a; Fromm, 1983; Gammelgaard & Lunn, 1997; Olsen, 2002; Rosenbaum, 1985).

Psychotherapy

There are different versions of psychotherapy, depending on which of the more specific theoretical schools in the psychodynamic field it is associated with. Like psychoanalysis, the aim of psychodynamic or psychoanalytical psychotherapy was healing, and it is founded on the idea that it comes through bringing the unconscious to consciousness and the consequent "inner reorganization". In psychotherapy, and here it is different from psychoanalysis, there is additionally an explicitly formulated objective of helping the patient. This part of the objective is fulfilled through a supportive attitude on the part of the therapist. Psychodynamic psychotherapy is founded on the same theoretical understandings as psychoanalysis. There might be schools and traditions of psychodynamic psychotherapy that set up different and more specific frameworks for the method and application of interpretations. Psychotherapy consists of conversations, in which the task of the therapist is to help the patient to become more able to understand and solve his or her problems. This means that the role of the therapist is different from that of the analyst. Where the analyst is neutral, the psychotherapist is more like the patient's professional friend or helper. The therapist plays a more active role in the process of understanding and solving than the analyst has in psychoanalysis. Traditionally, psychodynamic psychotherapy works through words and verbal expressions alone, since speech is regarded as the primary medium for consciousness and the formation of symbols. Psychodynamic psychotherapy is often regarded as "psychoanalysis light", but it is, in fact, different, and not simply a diluted form of psychoanalysis. The method requires the patient to attend frequent and regular therapy sessions, once or twice a week for a lengthy period such as a year.

Psychodynamic psychotherapy aimed originally at treatment, but, like psychoanalysis, it is sought by people who are not mentally ill, but feel a need for help to deal with certain difficult situations in life. The need arises typically in connection with major changes in life, such as marriage or partnership problems, divorce, a death in the family, problems with children, changes in roles in life, or chronic or transitory disease, unemployment, or persistent difficulties at work, or the like. People might also be facing existential problems, and thus need a private space to work them out, and in that way heighten their general robustness, capacity for reflection, and quality of life.

Psychodynamic coaching shares a common theoretical basis with psychotherapy, but is different from it in the working methods that can be used. In psychodynamic coaching, patients can be given "homework", asked to do drawings or write poems, or more structured tasks can be included, and more didactic steps can be taken that resemble instruction or information. Role-play or acting out scenes can also be introduced in psychodynamic coaching. Psychotherapy is a more regular and time-consuming method than coaching, and the time limit is not fixed from the start. Psychodynamic coaching focuses more than psychotherapy on the objective of the process. This does not mean that the process in psychodynamic coaching is less interesting, but that it is, to a greater degree, defined by the goal that has been set than the process in psychotherapy. In psychodynamic coaching, a goal is set up and used regularly for evaluation. The time limit is fixed from the start, in the hope that the client will take responsibility for reaching his or her goal within the allocated time. It is common to both psychotherapy and coaching that the development occurs through the relationship, and, therefore, the requirement for neutrality is also dropped here. The involvement with the client or patient and the relationship with the therapist is considered to be the most significant of the effective and healing factors (Cullberg, 1999; Olsen, 2002; Pedder, 1986; Rosenhan & Seligman, 1995). Couple therapy and family therapy are special types of psychotherapy, where the objective is to investigate the couple's dynamics for the purpose of helping them to solve their problems. Couple therapy and family therapy can be based on various understandings, as described in Chapter Four. From the starting point of psychodynamic system theory, the task is to investigate the projective processes together with the couple and understand them, so that the defences that bind the couple in conflicts can be resolved. Here, too, the therapist is the couple's or the family's "helper". The therapist is not on the side of either of the parties, and is in that way neutral. The coach does not take sides either, but, unlike the therapist, the coach is not neutral in relation to the content, since this must link up with the goal.

Group analysis

Group analysis is a method of analysing groups. The theory was originally formulated by Foulkes, who developed his theory and practice from his starting point in psychoanalysis. The fundamental principle in group analysis is that the group is the therapeutic medium through which the treatment and healing are carried out. Group analysis is therapy *of* the group, *in* and *by* the group. Therapy *of* the group means that the group as a whole is brought into the foreground as a unit, while the members form the background. This is what happens when the therapist discusses and interprets the way in which the group has acted as a whole, and disregards the fact that the individual members do not feel the same, or have contributed in different ways to the group matrix. Therapy *in* the group means that the individual members are brought into the foreground as the centre of focus, while the group as a whole forms the background. This happens when the therapist follows up on a member patient or speaks to one as an individual, and "forgets" the group for a while. *By* the group means that the members democratically make their own contributions and play an active part in the therapeutic process, through both their conscious and unconscious communications. The setting is a circle of chairs on which the members sit so that they can all see each other. One or two therapists will be associated with the group, and they sit in the circle.

Group analysis is carried on in regular sessions, usually once a week, and continues for a lengthy period. In slow-working open groups, the members might be replaced over time. A particular member might attend in the group for eighteen months, then leave it, and the empty place is taken by a new member. This provides the group with experience of integrating new members, with all the associated processes, and of parting with former members and saying goodbye to them. The method is free conversation, which means, as in psychoanalysis, free comments, associations, and reactions relating to "here and now". The therapists open the group conversation by saying "the discussion is open". Here, as in psychoanalysis, the therapists make use of their professional capacity for "freely floating attention", which is the way they gather "data" for the process of therapeutic interpretation.

Psychodynamic coaching in groups is different from group analysis, because of the different objectives, with regard to the time frame and the definition of goals. However, as can be seen from the appendix to the case in Chapter Five, "here and now" elements can also be included when coaching a group. This makes it possible to capture the group matrix, or the interplay between conscious and unconscious communication, and see the different dynamics between the members unfolding. Another major difference is that the members of the analysis group are either patients or professionals who are taking part as an element of their clinical training. Groups also exist with a mixture of members: patients, professionals in training, or people who, for the time being, have some aspect of their lives that they want to know more about. Group analysis is a very good way of learning about one's ability to form and maintain relationships. In group analysis, the therapist's interpretations—in the same way as in psychoanalysis and to some extent in psychotherapy—are not open to discussion. At this point, the methods are different from coaching, where the coach's interpretations and hypotheses can be discussed, since both the client and the coach are working on the task of investigation, though, admittedly, they each have their own sub-assignment and focus (Aagaard, Bechgaard, & Winther, 1994; Foulkes, 1984; Olsen, 2002).

Role analysis

Role analysis takes its starting point from the concept of roles. It is a relatively new method, and has been in the process of development during the past ten to fifteen years. On the way, it has pointed in slightly different directions. Krantz and Maltz (1997) created a model that they called ORC (organizational role consultation) with the central concepts of "role as given" and "role as taken". Hutton, Bazalgette, and Reed (1997) developed a model that they called ORA (organizational role analysis). Newton, Long, and Sievers (2006) have carried out further work on role analysis models. The method connects with the psychodynamic system theory, where the role is defined by the principal task, and where the role exists at the point where the individual and the organization meet. The same role will be played in different ways, depending on *who* is performing it. The aim of role analysis is to investigate the "organization in the mind" of the person in the role, which is the inner picture and the inner emotional idea of the organization and everything it contains. "Organization-in-the-mind" is built up from perceptions and inner emotional reality, which again is defined by the role history of the person performing the role, and his or her general makeup. The objective in this method is to uncover the client's "organization-in-the-mind", and is concerned with bringing the unconscious to conscious-ness within a limited area. The long-term objective in role analysis is to create greater freedom of action for the person in the role.

The work is done through conversation and drawings. The thera-pist or coach is called the consultant, and has an advisory and facili-tative function. Role analysis can be considered as a sub-set of psycho-dynamic coaching. In a sequence of coaching, one of the elements might be role analysis, but coaching could also bring other areas into focus besides the role at work. The domain of psychodynamic coach-ing is not exclusively working life and organizations. Private life can also be a centre of focus in psychodynamic coaching. Role analysis does not last as long as coaching. It could be completed in one or two sessions, for instance in connection with a conference at work or a course. This is the difference between the two methods, since psycho-dynamic coaching is a longer process and has broader objectives, while the coach's role and function are different from the consultant's.

Supervision

Supervision is a phenomenon originally associated with clinical train-ing of therapists and health care providers. Supervision means an overview, and the purpose of this overview is either to enable the ther-apist to be more skilful through case supervision, or to enhance the therapist's ability to see his or her own dynamics or those of the group or organization at work in a particular course of treatment. The aim of supervision is to create greater insight and understanding in the ther-apist. It has moved away from only occurring in learning contexts in clinical situations. Supervision has now spread to other areas of work-ing life, and to the educational sector, where the aim is more broadly to create insight for those who are supervised into their own ways of functioning and the effect it has on the problem situations they are dealing with. Supervision seeks to create greater insight, understood as a cognitive phenomenon, and to create greater awareness, which aims to bring the pre-conscious rather than the unconscious to consciousness. Supervision can be given to one or several people. Supervision in groups can draw in elements from group analysis. It is arranged as a process in which one or several of those being supervised present a case or a problem to the others, including the supervisor. They then examine the case closely in various ways through interviews or free discussion. One of the phenomena in focus during psychoanalytical supervision is the phenomenon of parallel processes. A parallel process is the designation for a situation in which the psychological content of the problem is recreated as the account of the problem is given. This means that feelings and positions that originate in the problem are gestalted in the now of the supervision and can be investigated there. Parallel processes might occur because unconscious material is transported by the speaker to the supervisor and any others being supervised, who will receive it in a different way from the speaker, and can, therefore, bring it into open reflection and interpretation. It could be said that this is one of the ways of working with transference and countertransference in supervision.

Psychodynamic coaching is different from supervision in its objective, its time frame, and in the role played by the supervisor or coach. Supervision and coaching are similar because in both situations it is possible to work through free or structured discussion (with a reflecting team, for example), and with drawings or acting out a situation. In several places, supervision has developed to include role analysis as one of the activities involved (Beck, 2004).

Psychodynamic coaching

The purpose of psychodynamic coaching is that the person being coached (the client), through acknowledgement and insight into his or her own history, personal patterns, inner structure, the present context and its dynamics, can combine past, present, and wishes for the future with realistic, feasible actions. Psychodynamic coaching takes its theoretical and conceptual starting point in psychodynamic theory concerned with personality and developmental psychology, couple psychology, social and group psychology, and psychodynamic system theory. The coaching is structured initially by defining a goal, and the procedure and structure of the course of coaching are agreed upon in relation to this goal. Coaching could be concerned with individuals, couples, organizational groups, or management groups. It might be started on a private initiative or as a total organizational action. To play the coach's part, it is necessary to be "personally committed through the role". This means: being present emotionally, with attention focused, registering with freely floating attention both to the client and to oneself, and striving to maintain the greatest possible freedom of relationship, while working in a neutral location and not reacting normatively. The coach's engagement consists of open, but timed, sharing of data that is relevant to the goal as countertransference, interpretations, hypotheses, observations, and associations. Several media can be used in the process: discussions, interviews, structured assignments, drawings, poems, and acting out situations. The process is regularly evaluated with reference to the initially defined goal, and then rounded off with an overall evaluation and summing up of the contributions of both parties and their joint efforts. Rounding off in this way makes it possible to take leave of each other, comment on one's own contribution and make any necessary adjustments, and to explain what was particularly important along the way.

Psychodynamic coaching

Name: _____

Date of request: _____ E-mail: _____

Telephone: _____ Mail: _____

Reference: _____

Special comments in connections to the request:

_____

_____

_____

Spontaneous thoughts, conceptions, ideas, and fantasies:

_____

_____

_____

_____

_____

_____

_____

Coaching

Date:	CRS: Mobile: E-mail:
Name:	
Address (private):	
Address (workplace/company)	
Marital status: Children:	
Special circumstances:	
Who pays:	
Request:	
Goal/object:	
Agreed-upon:	

APPENDIX 3

Data from the coaching sessions:	Reflections, associations, feelings, emotions, hypothesis, ideas . . .

Drawing assignment

Draw nine scenes from your life. There should be:

> three from your childhood;
> two from when you were young and growing up;
> two from your adult personal life;
> two from your present working life—one from before the present situation and one from the present situation.

They must show scenes that are important, either because they show how life typically was/is, or because they show situations that were, or came to be, especially important to you or in your life. This could be directly important, for example, if you were involved in an accident, lost someone or something, or it could have symbolic importance, for instance, such as something to do with your self-confidence or self-perception.

In other words, the scenes must illustrate an important story.

You will be given felt pens and paper. You need not worry about whether you are good at drawing or not. Draw as well as you can, but it is not the artistic aspect that is in focus.

Work structure for the designer team

09.00–10.30 Unstructured here-and-now session.

Task: To share feelings, fantasies and what we imagine.

Method: The discussion is open and everyone is encouraged to contribute. Who will start?

10.30–10.45 Break.

10.45–12.15 Theme assignment: How do we understand what is going on in this group?

The coach shares with the group what sees and observes, and her hypotheses with the group, who reflect together over the process in the first session and compare it with events in their everyday work.

12.15–13.00 Lunch.

13.00–14.30 Theme assignment: The personal story. One person tells the others his/her story, and the others must tell the group what feelings and thoughts came to them through listening to the story. They must also mention situations in the story that they could recognize from their own lives.

Finally, the one who told his/her story rounds off by saying what it has meant to him/her to tell the story and to listen.

14.30– 15.00   Break, when it was possible to withdraw (it is wearing to be so intense together for such a long time).

15.00–16.00   Conclusion: What has changed in my relations with the others after today? What could I personally learn from it? A joint round and reflection.

REFERENCES

Aagaard, S., Bechgaard, B., & Winther, G. (Ed.) (1994). *Gruppeanalytisk Psykoterapi*. Copenhagen: Hans Reitzels.

Agazarian, Y., & Peters, R. (1995). *The Visible and the Invisible Group*. London: Karnac.

Alderfer, C. P. (1987). An intergroup perspective on group dynamics. In: J. W. Lorsch (Ed.), *Handbook of Organizational Behaviour* (pp. 190–222). Englewood Cliffs, NJ: Prentice Hall.

Armstrong, D. (2005). *Organization in the Mind. Psychoanalysis, Group Relations, and Organizational Consultancy*. London: Karnac.

Beck, E. (2006). *Triadisk samspil hos mødre med borderline personligheds-forstyrrelse og deres spædbørn*. Copenhagen: Speciale fra Institut for Psykologi, Copenhagen Universitet.

Beck, U. C. (2004). Personligheden på arbejde: supervision i organisatorisk perspektiv. In: T. Heinskou & S. Visholm (Eds.), *Psykodynamisk Organisationspsykologi* (pp. 306–325). Copenhagen: Hans Reitzels.

Bering, E. (Ed.) (1989). *Hvad er psykoanalyse?* Copenhagen: Gyldendal.

Berne, E. (1967). *Games People Play*. Harmondsworth: Penguin.

Bion, W. R. (1961). *Experiences in Groups and other Papers*. London: Tavistock, 1985.

Bion, W. R. (1993). *Erfaringer i grupper*. Copenhagen: Hans Reitzels.

Blatner, A. (1996). *Acting-In: Practical Applications of Psychodramatic Methods*. New York: Springer.

Brenner, C. (1984). *Psykoanalysens grundbegreber*. Copenhagen: Hans Reitzels.

Brørup, M., Hauge, L., & Lyager Thomsen, U. (Eds.) (1993). *Psykologihåndbogen*. Copenhagen: Gyldendal.

Carver, C. S., & Scheier, M. F. (1992). *Perspectives on Personality* (2nd edn). Needham Heights, MA: Allyn and Bacon.

Cullberg, J. (1999). *Dynamisk Psykiatri*. Copenhagen: Hans Reitzels.

De Board, R. (1978). *The Psychoanalysis of Organisations*. London: Routledge.

Deegan II, A. X. (1979). *Coaching: A Management Skill for Improving Individual Performance*. Reading, MA: Addison-Wesley.

Dicks, H. V. (1967). *Marital Tensions. Clinical Studies Towards a Psychological Theory of Interaction*. New York: Basic Books.

Erikson, E. H. (1977). *Barnet og samfundet*. Copenhagen: Hans Reitzels.

Fonagy, P., Gergely, G., Jurist, E. L., & Target, M. (2007). *Affektregulering, mentalisering og selvets udvikling*. Copenhagen: Akademisk.

Foulkes, S. H. (1984). *Therapeutic Group Analysis*. London: Maresfield Reprints.

Freud, S. (1915e). The unconscious. *S.E.*, *14*: 161–215. London: Hogarth.

Freud, S. (1921c). *Group Psychology and the Analysis of the Ego*. *S.E.*, *18*: 67–143. London: Hogarth.

Freud, S. (1923b). *The Ego and The Id*. *S.E.*, *19*: 3–66. London: Hogarth.

Freud, S. (1933a). *New Introductory Lectures on Psycho-Analysis*. *S.E.*, *22*. London: Hogarth.

Fromm, E. (1983). *Freuds mission. En analyse af hans personlighed og indflydelse*. Copenhagen: Hans Reitzels.

Gabriel, Y. (1999). Psychoanalytic research into organizations. In: Y. Gabriel, L. Hirschorn, M. McCollom Hampton, H. S. Schwartz, & G. Swogger Jr (Eds.), *Organizations in Depth. The Psychoanalysis of Organizations* (pp. 251–280). London: Sage.

Gade, A. (2006). *Hjerneprocesser. Kognition og neurovidenskab* (5th edn). Copenhagen: Frydenlund.

Gammelgaard, J., & Lunn, S. (Ed.) (1997). *Om psykoanalytisk Kultur—et rum for refleksion*. Copenhagen: Dansk Psykologisk.

Habermas, J. (1981). *Theorie des kommunikative Handlens* (Vols. 1 & 2). Frankfurt: Suhrkamp.

Hansen-Skovmoes, P., & Rosenkvist, G. (2002). Coaching i organisationer. In: R. Stelter (Ed.), *Coaching—læring og udvikling* (pp. 85–106). Copenhagen: Psykologisk.

Heinskou, T., & Visholm, S. (Eds.) (2004). *Psykodynamisk Organisations-psykologi—på arbejde under overfladen.* Copenhagen: Hans Reitzels.

Hemmingsen, R. P., & Rosenberg, R. (1997). Bevidsthedsfysiologi, følelser og personlighed. *Ugeskrift for læger, 159*: 1067–1071.

Hinshelwood, R. D. (1991). *A Dictionary of Kleinian Thought.* London: Free Association Books.

Hirschhorn, L. (1995). *The Workplace Within. Psychodynamics of Organizational Life.* London: MIT Press.

Hirschhorn, L. (1999). Leaders and followers. In: Y. Gabriel, L. Hirschhorn, M. McCollom Hampton, H. S. Schwartz, & G. Swogger Jr. (Eds.), *Organizations in Depth. The Psychoanalysis of Organizations* (pp. 139–165). London: Sage.

Hirschhorn, L. (2000). Changing structure is not enough. In: Beer & Nohria (Eds.), *Breaking The Code of Change* (pp. 161–176). Boston, MA: Harvard Business School Press.

Huffington, C. (2006). A contextualized approach to coaching. In: H. Brunning (Ed.), *Executive Coaching. Systems–Psychodynamics Perspective* (pp. 41–78). London: Karnac.

Huffington, C., & Miller, S. (2008). Where angels and mere mortals fear to tread: exploring sibling relations in the workplace. *Organisational & Social Dynamics, 8*(1): 18–37.

Hustvedt, S. (2008). *En amerikaners lidelser.* Helsingør: Forlaget Per Kofod.

Hutton, J., Bazalgette, J., & Reed, B. (1997). Organisation-in-the-mind. In: J. E. Neumann, K. Kellner, & A. Dawson Shepherd (Eds.), *Developing Organisational Consultancy* (pp. 113–126). London: Routledge.

Jakobsen, P., & Visholm, S. (1987). *Parforholdet—Forelskelse, krise, terapi.* Copenhagen: Politisk Revy.

James, M., & Jongeward, D. (1976). *Født Vinder.* Copenhagen: Borgen.

Jaques, E. (1971). Social systems as a defence against persecutory and depressive anxiety. In: M. Klein, P. Heimann, & R. Money-Kyrle (Eds.), *New Directions in Pchycho-Analysis* (pp. 478–498). London: Tavistock.

Jaques, E. (1976). *A General Theory of Bureaucracy.* London: Heinemann.

Jennings, S. (1992). *Dramaterapi med familie, grupper og enkeltpersoner.* Copenhagen: Hans Reitzels.

Jensen, S. B., & Hejl, B. L. (1987). *Par i behandling.* Copenhagen: Munksgaard.

Jern, S., Boalt-Boëthius, S., Hidman, U., & Högberg, B. (1984). *Grupprelationer—en antologi om förhållandena mellan individ, grupp och organisation.* Stockholm: Natur och Kultur.

Jones, J. E., & Pfeiffer, J. W. (1973). *Strukturerede oplevelser til brug for træning i menneskelig samvirken* (Vols. 1, 2, & 3). Copenhagen: Teamco.

Jones, J. E., & Pfeiffer, J. W. (1979). *The Annual Handbook for Group Facilitators*. Los Angeles, CA: Los Angeles University Associates.

Jørgensen, C. R. (2002). *Psykologien i senmoderniteten*. Copenhagen: Hans Reitzels.

Katzenelson, B. (1994). *Homo Socius. Socialpsykologisk Grundbog*. Copenhagen: Gyldendal.

Kernberg, O. (1978). Leadership and organizational functioning. Organizational regression. *International Journal Group Psychotherapy, 28*: 3–25.

Kernberg, O. (1984). The couch at sea. The psychoanalysis of organizations. *International Journal Group Psychotherapy, 34*: 5–23.

Kernberg, O. (1994). Leadership styles and organizational paranoiagenesis. In: J. O. Ed & S. Bone (Eds.), *Paranoia: New Psychoanalytic Perspectives* (pp. 61–69). Madison, CO: International Universities Press.

Kernberg, O. (1998). *Ideology, Conflict and leadership in Groups and Organizations*. New Haven, CT: Yale University Press.

Klein, M. (1990). *Misundelse og taknemmelighed*. Copenhagen: Hans Reitzels.

Kohut, H. (1990). *Selvets psykologi*. Copenhagen: Hans Reitzels.

Krantz, J., & Maltz, M. (1997). A framework for consulting to organizational role. *Consulting Psychology Journal: Practice and Research, 49*(2): 137–151.

Kutter, P. (1982). *Basic Aspects of Pschoanalytic Group Therapy*. London: Routledge.

Mahler, M. S., Pine, F., & Bergman, A. (1975). *The Psychological Birth of the Human Infant*. New York: Basic Books.

Mead, G. H., & Morris, C. W. (Eds.) (1967). *Mind, Self and Society. From the Standpoint of a Social Behaviorist*. Chicago, IL: University of Chicago Press.

Menzies, I. E. P. (1975). A case study in the functioning of social systems as a defence against anxiety. In: A. D. Colman & H. Bexton (Eds.), *Group Relations Reader 1* (pp. 281–312). Washington: A. K: Rice Institute.

Miller, E. J., & Rice, A. K. (1975). Selections from systems of organizations. In: A. D. Colman & H. Bexton (Eds.), *Group Relations Reader 1* (pp. 43–68). Washington: A. K. Rice Institute.

Mortensen, K. (2001). *Fra neuroser til relationsforstyrrelser*. Copenhagen: Gyldendal.

Neumann, J. E., Kellner, K., & Dawson, S. (Eds.) (1997). *Developing Organisational Consultancy*. London: Routledge.

Newton, J., Long, S., & Sievers, B. (Eds.) (2006). *Coaching in Depth. The Organizational Role Analysis Approach.* London: Karnac.

Obholzer, A. (1994). Authority, power and leadership: contributions from group relations training. In: A. Obholzer & V. Roberts (Eds.), *The Unconscious at Work* (pp. 39–47). London: Routledge.

Olsen, O. A. (Ed.) (2002). *Psykodynamisk leksikon.* Copenhagen: Gyldendal.

Olsen, O. A., & Køppe, S. (1981). *Freuds psykoanalyse.* Copenhagen: Gyldendal.

Pedder, J. (1986). Reflections on the theory and practice of supervision. *Psychoanalytic Psychotherapy, 1:* 1–12.

Perls, F. S. (1973). *Gestaltterapi.* Copenhagen: Socialpædagogisk Bibliotek.

Rogers, C. (1971). *Om encountergrupper.* Copenhagen: Jespersen og Pios.

Rogers, C. (1992). *The characteristics of a helping relationship.* Boston, MA: Harvard Business School (Paper).

Rosenbaum, B. (Ed.) (1985). *Freud—efter Freud.* Copenhagen: FADL.

Rosenhan, D. L., & Seligman, M. (1995). *Abnormal Psychology.* New York: W. W. Norton.

Scharff, D. E., & Scharff, J. S. (1987). *Object Relations Family Therapy.* London: Jason Aronson, 1991.

Sjølund, A. (1965). *Gruppepsykologi.* Copenhagen: Gyldendals Pædagogiske Bibliotek.

Stelter, R. (Ed.) (2002). *Coaching—læring og udvikling.* Copenhagen: Psykologisk.

Stern, D. (1991). *Barnets interpersonelle univers.* Copenhagen: Hans Reitzels.

Tähkä, V. (1983). *Psykoanalytisk psykoterapi.* Copenhagen: Hans Reitzels.

Turner, J. C., & Reynolds, K. J. (2003). The social identity perspective in intergroup relations: theories, themes and controversies. In: R. Brown & S. L. Gaertner (Eds.), *Blackwell Handbook of Social Psychology: Intergroup Processes* (pp. 133–152). Oxford: Blackwell Publ. Ltd.

Visholm, S. (1993). *Overflade og dybde. Om projektiv identifikation og det modernesa psykologi.* Copenhagen: Politisk Revy.

Visholm, S. (2004). Par-og familieterapi. In: *GADs Psykologileksikon.* (s. 425–427). Copenhagen: GAD.

von Bertalanffy, L. (1968). *General System Theory. Foundations, Development and Application.* New York: George Braziller.

Waddington, C. H. (1957). *The Strategy of Genes.* London: Allen & Unwin.

Widlund, I. (Ed.) (1995). *Den analytiske gruppen. Gruppanalys i teori och praktik.* Stockholm: Natur och Kultur.

Willi, J. (1984). The concept of collusion—a combined systemic psychodynamic approach to marital therapy. *Family Process, 23:* 177–185.

INDEX

For Product Safety Concerns and Information please contact our EU
representative GPSR@taylorandfrancis.com
Taylor & Francis Verlag GmbH, Kaufingerstraße 24, 80331 München, Germany